Dedication

To Customers, everywhere.
God bless 'em!!

How to Eat an Elephant – About the Author

John Gilbert is a Yorkshireman who is married to Susan, with whom he produced two children who are now well grown. He lives in Rochdale in the United Kingdom and is a chemist by training.

He is a Fellow of the Royal Society of Chemistry (FRSC) and a Chartered Chemist (C.Chem).

He has worked for Akzo Chemicals for much of his career during which time he has performed a variety of duties ranging from R & D chemist, sales management, general management and more recently quality management. He has worked in several parts of the world including Canada, Holland and the United Kingdom.

Akzo Chemicals is a part of the Akzo Group of Companies with interests in chemicals, fibers, coatings and pharmaceutical products. In 1989 the company decided to use a quality management process from 3M Quality Management Services. John Gilbert implemented the model in the United Kingdom and Scandinavia and was responsible for much of the English adaptations necessary to the British culture.

He is a frequent, amusing and passionate speaker on the subject of quality improvement at seminars, symposia and training courses.

His well-known enthusiasm for his chosen work shines through in the pages of this book and will surely stimulate the reader to 'have-a-go' at Total Quality Management while providing lots of 'chuckles' on the way.

HOW TO EAT
AN ELEPHANT

a slice by slice guide to

TOTAL QUALITY
MANAGEMENT

John Gilbert

BROMLEY COLLEGE LIBRARY

WITHDRAWN

B05871

© J. Gilbert 1992

First published in Great Britain by Tudor Business Publishing Limited. Sole distributors worldwide, Hodder and Stoughton (Publishers) Ltd, Mill Road, Dunton Green, Sevenoaks, Kent, TN13 2XX.

British Library Cataloguing in Publication Data

Gilbert, John
  How to Eat an Elephant: Slice-by-slice
  Guide to Total Quality Management. –
  (Management Series)
  I. Title II. Series
  658.5

  ISBN 1–872807–80–1

All rights reserved. No part of this publication may be reproduced, stored in a retrieval system, or transmitted in any form or by any means, electronic, mechanical, photocopying, recording, or otherwise without prior permission of Tudor Business Publishing Ltd. at Stanton House, Eastham Village Road, Eastham, Wirral, Merseyside L62 8AD.

Typeset by Deltatype Ltd, Ellesmere Port, Cheshire.

Printed and Bound in Great Britain by Biddles Ltd.

Management
TQM
total quality management

BROMLEY COLLEGE OF TECHNOLOGY

ACCN.	58107 B 05871
CLASSN.	658.562
CAT.	LOCN.

Preface

This book has been written with the purpose of getting some fun from Total Quality Management (TQM), a continuous process of change made as dry as loft fluff by most of the people who write about it and teach it. If this book encourages you to try TQM then my goal has been scored, since after 30 years in business TQM has for me been a powerful breath of fresh air and some welcome common sense injected into an otherwise rather stuffy business world.

TQM has been almost ruined by 'quality' professionals who see it as a job for life so long as they keep it complicated. A better definition of TQM might be **Today Quit Moaning** and get on with improving things, it's not that difficult.

TQM is simple in concept and a powerful multi-faceted gem in action. There is no one single sparkling way to do it except to work at **conforming to your customers' expectations** by behaving in a way which makes it happen. I've met many Managing Directors who can understand this, well, at least a few!

I promise not to mention too often BS 5750 (ISO 9000), except to say that BS 5750 is about procedures, TQM is about people and both go well together, which is why it has been such a rich source of amusement to me.

There's not much structure to this book; you can open it anywhere, have a thought provoking read or a chuckle and shut it again. Most books on quality management run out of steam towards the end. This book is organised so that it runs out of steam in the middle; so start reading from either end! If you want a more structured approach, give me a call and I'll talk to you and yours. 'Why?', you might say, when you've already bought the book. Well, you can buy the Holy Bible for under £5, but ask yourself, 'How much more uplifting would the bible be if Jesus Christ himself would read it to me?'

John Gilbert, 1992

Acknowledgement

Many people encouraged me to write this book and provided much constructive criticism. In particular I would like to mention my colleagues Nico van Hoboken, Ian and Lesley Cookson, Dorothy Marshall, Mike Horsford and Lea and Arline Hopton. John Andrew Gilbert provided an insight into the practical aspects of Just-in-Time, motivation and the idea for 'The Sunday Lunch'. My grateful thanks to my wife, Susan for her encouragement and editorial assistance.

My gratitude also to 3M Quality Management Services who introduced me to the concepts, philosophy and the implementation of structured quality management, and to Akzo Chemicals for allowing me access to some material I have used when helping to position and implement the quality process in the company. Some of the images are from Presentation Task Force. Images copyright 1989, 1992.

So many other people have contributed to this book that it is impossible to mention them all. If I have forgotten to acknowledge anyone who made an unasked for contribution, I apologise. If you are inclined to sue, remember that this book is cheap, of low circulation and I live in my wife's house.

When Oscar Wilde was asked by the customs man, 'Have you anything to declare?', Oscar, the dear, replied, 'Only my genius'.

I don't even have that!

The HE/SHE syndrome

I was brought up on a diet of 'he' means 'he' or 'she' because Mrs Welsh, my English language teacher, told me that we've got no neuter in English. I'm not prejudiced against men, or women, for that matter. In fact, almost half the best people I know are men, and the other half are women, or thereabouts. In the book which follows, I have adopted a policy of half the references to the sex of people are women, and the other half are men. This seems fair and infinitely more sensible than using 'person' or 'he/she'.

Where people are mentioned in an unfavourable manner, they will in the main be men, and vice versa for women.

I do hope this satisfies about half my readers!!

Table of Contents

Slice 1 An Introduction to Elephant Eating

Whichever type of Total Quality Management you decide to practise, it is a process of change and has the characteristics:

- Focus on customer expectations.
- Prevention of problems.
- Building commitment to quality in the workforce.
- Open decision making.

However, the question is, 'How do you do it?'. That's easy, TQM processing is like eating an elephant. You do it in small, bite-sized chunks allowing plenty of time for chewing and digestion. Don't try to rush either eating an elephant or running a TQM process, it can't be done. TQM is about self-improvement and group-improvement through team building to better working practices. TQM is about the gradual change of people's behaviour towards the tasks they perform and their attitude towards other people. Run your process slowly to start, in small steps and often, allowing plenty of time for people to change their behaviour and when you feel discouraged, remember:

In the 90's, the competitiveness of any organisation will depend largely on continuous Quality Improvement using TQM Process methods and procedures that cover all functions, all activities and all your people. We are moving from an industrial society to an information society; from hierarchies to networks and from representative democracy to participative democracy. Some people might want to call this 'the new communism' or 'communalism'. It is certainly more effective than the adversarial business methods currently used because TQM involves all the people in the decision making process. Management personnel become responsible for managing CHANGE and not for DECIDING everything.

1.1 Sheep-Dipping

Whether or not you buy a TQM model, bear in mind that most organisations are not academic institutions and the people who work for you are interested in practice, not theory. TQM needs some rhetoric because people need a principle or two to get excited about. But make sure your TQM process is clear about the ACTIONS to take.

At a seminar, I listened to a well-known company representative pull the wool over ignorant eyes about their magical quality results, when I know that the model full of rhetoric this organisation purchased four years before, simply 'sheep-dipped' the people in 'quality-speak'. They waited two years for the 20% improvement they expected and nothing happened. They started again with a process shorter on talk and longer on action. However, the rhetoric had helped to put the rocket on the launch pad and get the engines started. When the quality 'action' process started, only a small boost made the whole process take off.

'Sheep-dipping' raises expectations but without 'action' you simply create frustration, because the people don't know what to do.

Slice 2 Types of Quality Process

There are three basic types of quality model, Process Analysis, Integrated and Charismatic. Each of the processes focuses on the customer in order to determine what actions the organisation should take to improve itself. However, the structure and organisation of the TQM processes used to achieve these actions differ substantially.

Many aspects of each of the three processes are similar and all merge into one when excellence has been achieved.

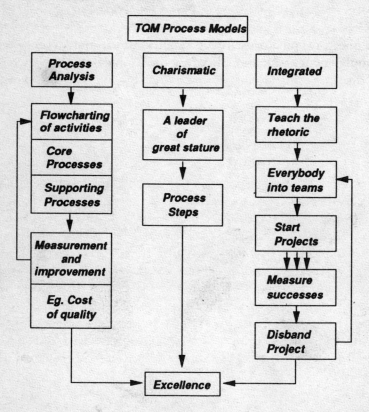

2.1 Process Analysis TQM

Process analysis is just that, analysing the activities of the

4

processes of your business in a search for a better understanding of where improvement can be made. The Core and Supporting processes of the business should be identified and flow charts prepared showing the interlinks between them. Inputs and outputs to each of the processes are defined, plus customers and suppliers, responsibilities, interfaces and actions.

Process analysis is essentially a top-down process of improvement with reviews from the bottom-up. Identifying who is the process owner is an essential requirement and nothing of value will likely happen until the process owner is found. The owner is often an elusive character and may well initially deny responsibility for his *own* process, but lay claim to somebody else's process!

The method of implementing this type of process is described in Slice 33.

2.2 Charismatic TQM

Charismatic TQM is less structured and is typified by companies such as Disney and Marks and Spencer. When they were small outfits, they had leaders with vision who infused a sense of quality and pride of belonging in all the people, since they were small enough for the leader to know everybody.

Charismatic TQM is also typified by my local butcher! He is there, with his staff, all day, every day, 'massaging' and serving his customers. He doesn't need a fancy manual to describe his quality policy, vision and mission in life. He shows it all day and every day to his people and his customers. The question is, could he infuse the same sense of continuous excellence in his operations if he had five or six butcher's shops spread around the town?

2.3 Integrated TQM.

Integrated TQM is an 'all fronts' process based upon teams at all levels.

5

The focus remains on the customers' expectations and the prevention of problems, but with this type of TQM process model, the method of accomplishing the actions is to organise people into teams from the top to the bottom of the organisation. These include steering teams, quality circles, facilitator networks and various types of project teams.

This involvement in teams and team-work is highly motivating, can be great fun, and builds commitment to quality in the workforce. More details on the implementation of this type of process is given in Slice 34.

Slice 3 Quality Process Definitions

If we are to make a reasonable job of dealing with our slice by
slice approach to elephant eating, then a few definitions are in
order.

3.1 Quality Definition

A committee of quality boffins decided for the purposes of the
ISO 8402–1986: Quality-Vocabulary Standard, that Quality is
defined as:

> *The totality of features and characteristics of a
> product or service that bear on its ability to
> satisfy stated or implied needs.*

What a mouthful, the average telephone receptionist (your
front line to the market place) will never remember that. Teach
her something a bit shorter and hopefully more exciting. How
about a definition that is often quoted because it comes from a
Guru, Mr Juran? He defined quality as Fitness for Purpose.
What's wrong with that? I'll tell you, Fitness for Purpose is not
easily measurable. However, the definition of quality which I
prefer is:

Consistent conformance
to customers'
expectations

7

This definition can be measured directly by asking customers regularly how satisfied they are. The quality professionals have much to answer for. Let's hope they don't overhaul their views any more. There are enough book length dissertations on the definition of quality already. Keep your quality definition simple, so that everybody can understand it and make sure the customers keep coming back, and not the product. The only way to do this is to 'consistently conform to your customers' expectations'.

The real fault with so many quality definitions I read is that they do not mention either *customers* or *efficiency*. How can you meet your own expectations or those of the customer unless efficiency improvement is stated or implied in your quality definition?

But don't ever imply the word *customer* in your quality definition, actually use the word, it won't hurt!

3.2 Total Quality Definition

I'm not sure how useful a bunch of definitions can be, but since we are on the subject, of the many definitions of Total Quality I have seen, I believe the best is:

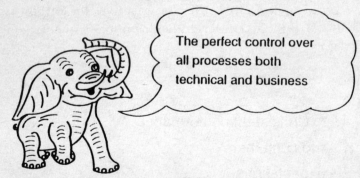

The perfect control over all processes both technical and business

But what happens when we add the word 'management' to Total Quality? The main effect is to imply that choices can now be made about total quality. The usual choice is to focus total quality in the direction of the customer and towards problem prevention rather than inspection.

A good quantitative definition of Total Quality Management is:

> **A process designed to focus on customer expectations, preventing problems, building commitment to quality in the workforce and promoting open decision making.**

The value of defining TQM is that it encompasses the overall goal in general terms of what you are trying to accomplish and provides a building block for your more specific Vision Statement (Slice 4) and Critical Success Factors (Slice 35).

Slice 4 Vision Statement and Quality Policy

Some organisations, particularly those which practise 'charismatic' TQM, combine the Vision Statement and Quality Policy.

Go for a simple one if you can, like Disney:

We're in the business of making people happy.

or Avis Rent-a-Car:

We try harder

The advantage of these simple combined statements is that they are memorable.

4.1 Vision Statement

More and more organisations that use structured TQM models separate their Vision Statement and Quality Policy.

A Vision Statement comes from the top of the organisation and says how it wants to be perceived at some future time. It is the goal for everyone in the organisation and makes legitimate their right to contribute to improvements. A Vision Statement should be possible, authentic, compelling and make you feel good.

 As the One Minute Manager[5] puts it, a Vision (goal) should be SMART which means Specific, Measurable, Attainable, Relevant and Trackable.

A Vision Statement shows the direction in which to go and is a tool to position the customer's perception of the organisation and, of course, the organisation's image of itself. It does not define the methodology for getting there. That is the purpose of the organisation's Quality Policy.

Some people hold the view that a Vision Statement should convey the vision of the organisation in a short snappy statement such as 'Delighting the Customer' or 'Encircle Caterpillar' (Komatsu, a manufacturer of earth moving equipment).

Whichever way you view it, a Vision Statement is there to set a course and a goal and show the purpose of the long haul of quality improvement.

4.2 Quality Policy

To run a successful TQM process you need a Quality Policy.

You need a quality policy which is memorable, but not necessarily comprehensive, otherwise, nobody will be able to remember it.

A quality policy is needed to provide guidance to your people about how to accomplish the Vision decided by the president. It places limits on the actions of everybody. If you do not want them to make 3-wheeler cars, say so in your quality policy by making it utterly clear what you do want them to do and the principles of how you want them to do it.

Slice 5 Visible TQM

Don't keep your TQM process secret. 'Ridiculous', you say, 'I talk about it often.' Yet it may still seem a secret to some people. The boss talks to Heads of Department, who, as middle line managers, haven't the time for TQM and never talk to their people about it. If there is nothing to see around the place, the people will think the process is dead, even though you are hoarse through volubility.

Keep TQM visible. Door mats with quality messages, framed messages, posters, flags, product packaging stickers, quality pins, recognition certificates on walls and corporate clothing. Put messages on blotters, diaries, visiting cards (I know of one company who print their Vision Statement on the back of their visiting cards), pay slips, and envelopes.

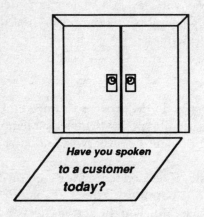

The list of possible ways to make your process visible is endless. One of my favourites is to put up measurement charts of non-sensitive issues on notice boards. After all, it is done for safety records.

There are thousands of factories with a sign at the entrance that says *This site has worked ‹350› accident free days*. Why not do the same type of thing for quality improvement?

Use posters carefully. Unless they are properly positioned, changed regularly and have some significance that people

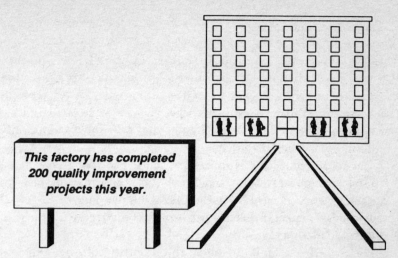

immediately and personally identify with, they become part of the furniture.

To test this, put up a useful poster and three weeks later, go ask a few people what it says. Most of them will not be able to tell you.

Slice 6 Customers

Quality has many customers, so it is as well to know who they are. To most people the customer is the person or organisation who receives the goods and services provided. This is too broad a definition. We need a sub-division; the *internal customer* and the *external customer*, the latter being the one most commonly identified as 'the customer'.

Since our objective is to *conform to our customers' expectations*, then it becomes essential to achieve this conformation for both internal and external customers. Conforming to external customers' expectations is a push-over compared with those of internal customers.

We need not labour over the identity of the external customers; she is the 'boss', the one who ultimately pays our wages and her identity should be known from your business strategy and marketing processes, but internal customers are often less obvious. Try to focus on individuals; saying that the production department or the finance department is your customer, is not personal enough. Who is the person upon whom your personal product or service impacts? He or she is the person to whom you should go to find out if you are, or are not, conforming to his or her expectations.

6.1 Customer Expectations

'Wants' and 'needs' are related but not entirely the same. Expectations is the combination of written specifications and emotional needs and wants. Of course, expectations have to be reasonable, but it is up to you to make sure the customer knows what she can expect, after which you conform to these expectations, every time.

When you buy a new washing machine, you expect that it not only works, but that the price is right, it is delivered on time, and that it looks good. These are expectations which extend well beyond the requirement that the machine works.

'I've got 500 washing machines out there', said the

14

production manager, 'and we've put a British electrical plug on them but they are for export to Holland. They all work OK, but the Quality Control department won't pass them. Will you?'

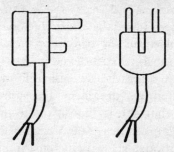

'Certainly', said the Managing Director, 'but first get me the specification sheet so I can write on it that they can't be connected to the Dutch electricity supply. Will that do?'

'Er, well I suppose not,' said the production manager.

Compromise will not do.

A few slices, yes?

Slice 7 Customer Relations

Customers can be a nuisance, right? They disturb the priorities we have set for ourselves and force us to do things in an order we had not planned for. This is a common malaise of companies who are not organised for the benefit of their customers.

Adversarial relationships can develop between supplier and customer to the extent that sales people refer to customers as *my* customers rather than *our* customers. The sales person does this because she feels that she is the only one on the side of the customer. The organisation is not. Very unhealthy.

Some organisations see their customers as intrusive nuisances who demand reassurance by inspecting not only the goods delivered but also the quality of the supplier's organisation. They ask searching questions and are generally seen to *intrude* on the suppliers' personal affairs.

The only acceptable attitude from a 'quality' supplier is to welcome the customer when he wants to know not only what you do but also how you do it. This is a *partnership* relationship where both supplier and customer expect to learn from each other (Slice 92).

Practising effective TQM gradually moves the relationship from adversarial or intrusive to a partnership, for the good of both sides.

7.1 Guarantees

A result of doing it right every time is that you are better able to provide guarantees and warranties for your product or service which possess real 'umph'. You may go so far as to guarantee to penalise yourself if you fail to meet your customer's expectations. This is helpful to your market position since competitors may not have the same level of confidence in their service as you have in yours.

Meaningful guarantees of product or service can help develop an edge on the competition because you are distinguished from them.

16

I am reminded of a well-known pizza delivery service. They say, 'If the pizza is not delivered within 30 minutes, it's free.' They actually do deliver inside 30 minutes.

However, I understand they also have 22 law suits pending from injured pedestrians. . . .

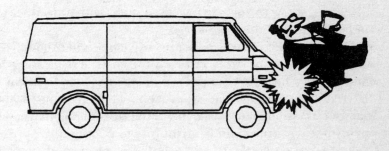

Slice 8 The Quality Gurus

A guru is defined as a good man, a wise man, a teacher. They also tend to be charismatic characters, often well ahead of their time who contribute significantly to their chosen field. In spite of criticism and occasional ridicule, people destined to be deified as gurus will stick to their guns because they are sincere and often passionate about their beliefs.

In the world of 'quality', the gurus fit this general description, and are usually categorised according to their geographical origin. There are lots of them, although a few stand out as pioneers[2].

The gurus have contributed the thinking and practise to the quality improvement movement in two way. Some of them concentrated on the *philosophical* aspects of quality improvement and others concentrated on the *tools of quality*. However, in all cases they were and are practical men, with a deep seated understanding of the *common man*.

They understood the need for improvements in productivity and efficiency in order to reduce unit costs and in order for industries to survive. Cost reduction was not seen by them as the old 'time-and-motion' approach. They recognised that waste of time and materials, demeaning rules and management ineptitude were the main contributors to poor quality.

It was not necessary to pay people less or make them work harder through various forms of fear. On the contrary, the gurus recognised that the most valuable resource of an organisation was its people, and the people are motivated and work best when they are valued, encouraged to contribute and allowed to make their own decisions.

The Early Americans

W Edwards Deming	Management philosophy
Joseph M Juran	Planning and Quality Costs
Armand V Feigenbaum	Total Quality Control

The Japanese

Kaoru Ishikawa   Tools
                             Quality Circles
                             Company-wide quality.

Genichi Taguchi   Minimum Prototyping

Shigeo Shingo   Poka-Yoke (Zero Defects)

The Westerners

Philip B Crosby   Awareness
                             Zero Defects
                             Do it right first time.

Tom Peters   Customer Orientation

Claus Møller   Personal Quality

They disagree on many peripheral issues, but all agree that TQM is a *management-led*, never ending process in which *top management commitment* is essential.

Summary of the guru teachings

- Management commitment and involvement are essential. Management has an obligation to lead the quality process without which little will happen.
- Make relevant measurements which state the current situation and set goals.
- Encourage and train people in team-work and problem solving which should include simple tools of quality improvement which people can use. The effect is commitment to quality improvement and the promotion of open decision making. Team construction methods should emphasise the need to break down inter-departmental barriers.
- In addition to the simple tools of quality there are many systems based tools that can improve productivity. For example, Just-in-Time techniques.

- Prevention is better than inspection. It is better to design the product or system in such a way that the possibility of error is reduced or eliminated.
- Quality improvement should be customer focused. There are both internal customers and external customers and all of them are equally important.

Slice 9 The Early American Gurus

They took the quality message to the Japanese after the second world war, because, ironically, they were not listened to at home, which is a great pity.

9.1 W Edwards Deming

He introduced the concept of 'variance' to the Japanese and a systematic approach to problem solving which eventually was called the PDCA cycle (Plan, Do, Check, Act). Later he pushed the need for management involvement and produced his now famous *14 points*.[22].

1. *Create constancy of purpose to improve product and service.*
2. *Adopt new philosophy (management learning and leadership).*
3. *Cease dependence on inspection. . . .*
4. *End awarding business on price. . . .*
5. *Improve constantly and forever the system of production and service. . . .*
6. *Institute training on the job.*
7. *Institute leadership. . . .*
8. *Drive out fear so that all may work effectively for the organisation.*
9. *Break down barriers between departments. . . .*
10. *Eliminate slogans, exhortations and numerical targets. . . .*
11. *Eliminate quotas or work standards, and management by objectives or numerical goals; substitute leadership.*
12. *Remove barriers that rob people of their right to pride of workmanship. . . .*
13. *Institute a vigorous education and self-improvement programme.*
14. *Put everyone in the company to work to accomplish the transformation.*

9.2 Joseph Juran

Like Deming, Juran was very influential in Japan during the 1950's. He wrote many books, and in the one entitled *The Economics of Quality* he coined the now famous phrase 'There is gold in the mine' (Slice 25) to capture the idea that problems can be used as sources of improvement. In his later years he transferred much of his attention away from the technical issues of quality. He began to talk about management's responsibility for quality and the need to set goals and targets for improvement. He taught that quality control should be conducted as an integral part of management control.

He said that quality does not happen by accident, it must be planned; he developed a 9-point 'Quality Planning Road Map' and he was sceptical about the value of quality circles and 'zero-defect' concepts.

In summary, his main foci are:

(1) Quality Control to be an integral part of Management Control,
(2) Top quality is no accident.
(3) Quality must be planned.
(4) There are no shortcuts to the achievement of total quality.

He propounded the concept of the *Quality Trilogy; Planning, Control and Improvement.*

9.3 Armand Feigenbaum

He believes in total quality control where a systematic approach should be used involving all the functions of the organisation and not just manufacturing. Quality should be built in at an early stage and the system should be allowed to develop gradually. He sees quality improvement as the single most important force leading to organisational success and growth.

He originated the concept of Total Quality Control. He says 'Quality is in its essence a way of (completely) managing the organisation' and requires,

(1) a clear understanding of international markets,
(2) that management needs a thorough grasp of total quality strategy with a hands-on style and
(3) that total quality processes are the single most powerful change agent for companies today.

22

Slice 10 The Japanese Gurus

10.1 Kaoru Ishikawa

The late Dr. Ishikawa, who was Emeritus Professor of The University of Tokyo, first began surveying and studying quality control when he joined a research group set up by the Union of Japanese Scientists and Engineers (JUSE) in 1949. He lectured and consulted on quality improvement and quality control all over the world.

In 1949 Kaoru Ishikawa was the first to recognise that quality improvement is too important to leave in the hands of specialists. He said it should be company-wide from board-room to back-room, top to bottom and an all pervasive influence on the way business is conducted.

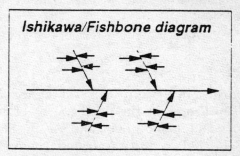

Ishikawa/Fishbone diagram

Like other quality tools, he used the cause-and-effect diagram to great effect as a device to assist groups (quality circles) with their improvement efforts. The diagram often bears his name and is a useful way to find, sort out and document the causes of variation of quality.

He has made three main contributions to quality.

(1) The use of simplified technical tools (the 7 tools of Quality Control, Slice 48) to be used by all the people of the organisation.
(2) He contributed to the concept of Quality being a company-wide issue.
(3) The Quality Circle Movement in Japanese companies.

10.2 Genichi Taguchi

He developed a methodology for minimum prototyping in product design and trouble shooting in production. The methodology is concerned with the routine optimisation of product and process prior to manufacture, rather than the use of inspection as a tool of quality. The design aspects of off-line quality control are divided into three stages: *System Design, Parameter Design* and *Tolerance Design*.

System design is the art of creating a design concept or 'an up and limping' prototype. Parameter design is the crucial step and involves testing the design features in order to find the ones that are least sensitive to outside changes. Tolerance design is then applied to reduce variations further. If necessary, better raw materials or equipment will be purchased.

This type of thinking reflects the Japanese philosophy of 'invest last not first'.

10.3 Shigeo Shingo

Shigeo Shingo died in November 1990 at the age of 81 and was one of the key figures in the development of Just-in-Time Manufacturing and its promotion and use outside Japan. He was one of the 20th century's greatest engineers and was honoured by the whole world for the major contributions he made, not only to the thinking process behind quality improvement, but also the methodology of the processes.

He is best remembered for his work on the development of Quick Changeover (SMED) and Mistake-Proofing (Poka Yoke). He said himself that he would prefer to be remembered for his promotion of the understanding necessary behind the concepts and practise of looking at the total manufacturing process and the elimination of transportation, storage, lot delays and inspection.

The Poka-Yoke system (mistake proofing or 'Defect=0') for production processes is based on the use of preventive measures. Shigeo Shingo said that the process should be stopped whenever a defect occurs, exhaustively investigated and steps taken to elaborate the cause and prevent the reoccurrence of the defect by eliminating the cause. This requires constant monitoring of potential error sources so as to nip them in the bud before they become a problem. His work has been associated with many successful Just-in-Time systems.

He also worked on machine set-up time reduction for engineering companies to develop methods of reducing or minimising set-up time. This methodology is known as Single Minute Exchange of Die (SMED).

Slice 11 The Western Gurus

11.1 Philip Crosby

He is well known for the concepts of Do It Right First Time and Zero Defects. He bases his quality improvement methods on the Four Absolutes of Quality Management:

(1) Conformance to requirements.
(2) Prevention not appraisal.
(3) Zero Defects.
(4) Measurement of the Price of Non-conformance.

In addition he has Fourteen Steps to Quality Improvement as the method of implementing the process. They are:

1. Management commitment.
2. Form quality improvement teams.
3. Measure to find improvement areas.
4. Evaluate the cost of quality.
5. Raise quality awareness.
6. Take actions to correct problems.
7. Establish progress monitoring of the improvement process.
8. Train supervisors.
9. Hold a 'Zero-Defect' day.
10. Encourage people to establish improvement goals.
11. Encourage people to tell management about the obstacles they face.
12. Recognise and appreciate those who participate.
13. Establish quality councils to communicate on a regular basis.
14. Do it all over again.

11.2 Tom Peters

He emphasises the importance of customers, innovation, people, leadership and systems. He sees leadership rather than management as the central issue behind quality improvement and is an advocate of Management by Walking About (MBWA, Slice 20) as a mechanism for:

- Listening (caring)
- Teaching (value transmission) and,
- Facilitating (helping).

He is the guru who talks most about customers and in his third book, *Thriving on Chaos,* deals with each key area in terms of 'prescriptions' as the way to bring about the necessary 'Management Revolution'.

11.3 Claus Møller

He developed the concept of Personal Quality as the central element of TQM. He talks about the 12 Golden Rules to aid quality improvement:

1. Set personal quality goals.
2. Establish own personal quality account.
3. Check how satisfied others are with your efforts.
4. Regard the next link as a valued customer.
5. Avoid errors.
6. Perform tasks more effectively.
7. Utilise resources well.
8. Be committed.
9. Learn to finish what you start.
10. Control your stress.
11. Be ethical.
12. Demand quality.

He also has the 17 Hallmarks of a quality organisation. He emphasises administrative procedure improvement rather than the improvement of production processes. He further emphasises the use of check lists and the two standards of personal quality; Ideal Performance level (IP) and Actual Performance level (AP). Overall, he believes in people improvement as the key to quality improvement.

Slice 12 The Process of Change

TQM is about managing the process of change. Most of us do not welcome change and prefer not to change. It disturbs our daily equilibrium; it forces us to think and take decisions. But without change the human race would be deadly dull and nothing would ever get any better, or worse for that matter. The most important change taking place inside an effective TQM process is the changing behaviour of people.

12.1 Behaviour Change

Despite extensive training in quality awareness, Statistical Process Control, BS 5750 (ISO 9000), who can say that they personally changed their behaviour in the sense of 'doing things right first time'. When was the last time you were about to embark upon a routine task and asked yourself, 'Can I do this right first time every time?' If not, ask yourself, 'What can I improve or fix before I start?'.

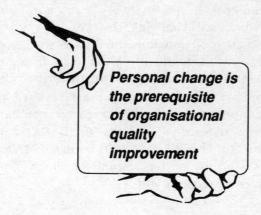

Personal change is the prerequisite of organisational quality improvement

This personal change involves both major and minor activities, but starts with the minor ones. Improve the way you manage your bench or your desk. Don't live any longer with the telephone in the wrong place, or a pile of paper which should be filed. Do something about it, now! Eat your elephant, one piece

29

at a time. The major changes start to come about when you have a Vision in place and a plan. Of course, *nothing* will change if you are entirely satisfied with the way conditions are at present. But don't be stubborn about it; you and yours can almost certainly improve and all it requires is the right attitude and the right actions.

Message: Quality improvement is about deciding to tackle problems. Train people to see problems as goldmines for improvement and foster an atmosphere of open decision making. This will change their attitude and behaviour towards their work and quite ordinary people will begin to move mountains. It requires a sensitive touch, patience and understanding particularly from management personnel.

12.2 Facilitating Change

The changes needed to the behaviour of the people and the organisation need to be facilitated from within, using your own people, often called facilitators (Slice 43). Your facilitators should be familiar with the workings of the organisation.

You know what needs changing when you have clear goals to aim for and when you know how the organisation works. For example, BS 5750 (ISO 9000), provides a framework for making changes without causing chaos by writing down the procedures you use to make things happen in your business.

It is no use simply deciding what to change, you have to set deadlines, review dates, goals and measurement criteria (Slice 37); you have to DO IT and put yourself under some reasonable pressure by setting completion dates. You might say this is a lack of freedom, but:

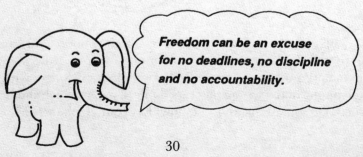

Freedom can be an excuse for no deadlines, no discipline and no accountability.

Planned, systematic follow-up of activities becomes a predominant feature of your TQM process and serves to continually emphasise your commitment to quality improvement. Regular follow-up also serves to show clearly that quality improvement is a *process* and not a *programme* and that it will not go away.

Slice 13 Quality Assurance

Lionel Stebbing[21], used a Wagnerian analogy to describe quality assurance from the philosophy of *Gesamtkunstwerk* (complete art work). When Wagner worked on a musical drama, before he completed the music, he gave much thought to the words, costumes, scenery and overall presentation before he finalised the music. His intention was always to create a complete sound picture.

Quality Assurance uses this philosophy and is the assembly of all functions and activities that bear upon the quality of a product or service so that all are treated equally, planned, controlled and implemented in a systematic manner.

In the late 20th century we are rediscovering, re-defining and using principles of craftsmanship from the distant past and then calling it quality assurance. Ming vases have lasted so well because nothing was left to chance in their creation.

In the late 19th century, operators controlled quality, but in the early 20th century, foremen controlled quality. Unfortunately, foremen were given responsibility for the craftsmens' work without necessarily knowing how to do it themselves, so by the 1920's we needed quality control inspectors.

What utter nonsense! It gets worse. By the 1940's the situation had reached such a pitch of poor quality through loss of craftsmanship, foremen with bigger egos than ability and an

32

'inspection' mentality, that we had to invent statistical quality control to make further progress. The adoption of ISO 9000 principles, Total Quality Management and quality assurance has gradually allowed us to return to craft principles suitable for mass production of goods and services.

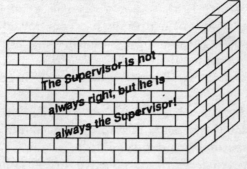

The Supervisor is not always right, but he is always the Supervisor!

Unfortunately, all too few organisations really practise these principles, but ISO 9000 will certainly help. We should return to some of the original principles of craftsmanship like 'apprenticeship' and 'on-the-job-training'. These methods built excellence, pride and continuity of quality. The people who bought these crafted goods knew they were paying more, and didn't mind because the goods were worth it.

Have you seen the price of a *Ming* vase lately!!

Slicing nicely, yes?

Slice 14 ISO 9000

ISO 9000 is a stepping stone along the road to Total Quality Assurance and to Total Quality Management.

ISO 9000 (BS 5750), is an international standard for quality systems. It does not guarantee good quality and indeed allows you to institutionalise your mistakes if you so wish. In the end, customer pressure will make you do it, which is a shame because all enterprises should want to conform to ISO 9000 principles and practises without the need for external pressure.

What it does for you is to force you to write down what you do and it brings the benefits of improved accountability, traceability, consistency and discipline of action. These are all laudable characteristics of effective organisations and, of course, management people believe in them. However, we often label them as 'important but not urgent'. The intention to seek ISO 9000 registration pushes these important characteristics into the urgent box, and finally something gets done about them.

The ISO 9000 Standard is a definition for a quality management system. When all the key procedures have been written down and understood, the standard has provided a framework for making changes without causing chaos. During the development of quality manuals for ISO 9000 registration, while top managers were reading the procedures, how many said things like:

34

Similar, and frequently repeated questions in the board-rooms of European companies are other questions, such as:

Question: 'Surely, we don't do that?'

Question: 'Why on earth do we do that?'

Question: 'I thought we'd stopped doing that years ago?'

The ISO 9000 series of standards grew out of military standards and various other procurement standards.

- ISO 9003 is concerned with final inspection and testing only.
- ISO 9002 includes everything in ISO 9003 plus production and installation.
- ISO 9001 includes the other two standards plus design/development.

ISO 9000 Structure

Level 1. Policy Manual. Contains definitions, policies and the method of approach.
Level 2. List of Procedures. These are flow diagrams or descriptions which identify the process owner and control the critical steps.
Level 3. Work procedures. How things are done.
Level 4. Records.

Helpful Hints when embarking on registration.

- Decide on an achievable level of quality.
- Get everyone involved and don't forget to include off-site activities.
- For large organisations, appoint a full time Quality Assurance coordinator and don't use a consultant.
- Tell yourself the truth, don't make things up; keep it simple and don't send copies of everything to everyone.
- Only calibrate quality critical instruments.
- Delegate control of Level 3 and use it for methods and recipes.

Slice 15 TQM Takes Time

Learning a system for quality improvement, organising for quality improvement and even planning for quality improvement can all be put in place within an organisation fairly quickly. Say, 2 years for a large organisation of several thousand people with committed and involved management. These phases will take longer or not happen at all if top management delegates the activities.

Achieving quality improvement in terms of improved customer satisfaction and a meaningful reduction in waste of time and physical resources, takes longer still. I refuse the temptation to say how many years, because I don't know. But one thing is for sure, the behaviour change that results from the constant practise of this management led revolution takes even longer. It will be ten years before the attitude of 'only right-first-time will do' is institutionalised in the organisation. Let's look at the phases.

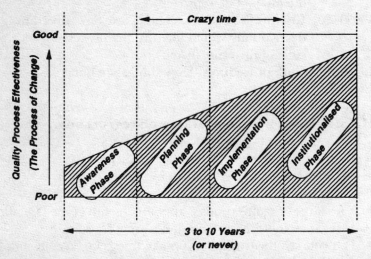

The Awareness Phase is when you are teaching the rhetoric of the process and encouraging people to discuss it and generally making them aware that there are possible shifts in the paradigm to be had.

36

The Planning Phase involves organising everybody into teams, developing annual quality plans and deciding on project improvement priorities.

The Implementation Phase is when all the people go through the agony of diverting their attention away from the day to day activities of the job to spending a meaningful amount of time on improvement.

The Institutionalised Phase is when the quality improvement process methodology and thinking are axiomatic and people begin to say, 'whatever happened to all that stuff we used to do on quality 'n' years ago?'

The four phases are not of equal length; some organisations do a particular phase more quickly than others. But it is certain that it takes a lot of time, because the behaviour of people is changing through ACTIONS. There are lots of setbacks, restarts, frustrations and re-definitions. At times the organisation will feel rather schizophrenic (crazy time), but the change does happen in the end and the process of improvement becomes continuous.

15.1 Institutionalised TQM

What does institutionalised mean? It means:

- When the process has reached perpetual motion.
- When you see the look of surprise and despondency on the face of a new starter when you tell him it will be three months before he's any use.

- When anyone can stand up and give a 15 minute presentation about quality improvement in their department.
- When anyone can be trusted to talk to an external customer.
- When the quality improvement process can survive a change of boss!!

Slice 16 Quality Culture

Culture is something that we mess with at our peril, or so I'm told. The dictionary definition of culture is, 'trained and refined understanding of manners and taste . . .' This doesn't seem to me to be so fancy that we can't aspire to change it gradually where it needs changing. However, it is ill-advised to tell people that you are going to change their culture because you are implying that they do not think and act correctly.

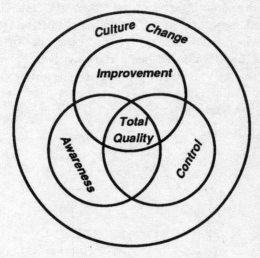

No problem. Start with changing working practices for the better. This will in time alter people's behaviour and their culture will go along with it.

Since it seems to upset people so much when you say you are going to change their culture, I always say in teaching workshops that the quality process won't interfere with their culture. I tell them, 'I'm a Yorkshireman, defined as a Scotsman stripped of his natural generosity, and nobody is going to stop me being mean.' It seems to make them feel better. God knows why, but at least it gives them a 'chuckle-point'.

If you operate in several European countries, then:

16.1 Personal Quality

Who's responsible for quality? Well, she is, he is, they are or someone is. In truth, I am, you are, we all are. Quality improvement starts with individual people deciding to do things better.

When was the last time you spent a minute, or an hour, or a day, improving something before you started a task. How often have you said something like, 'I must sort out that telephone wire around the inside of the table leg so I can get the telephone nearer to my hand.' You've been living with the problem for months or years. You know how to fix it but it takes five minutes. Every time you pick up the telephone it costs an extra second. The payback on your improvement time could be very rapid.

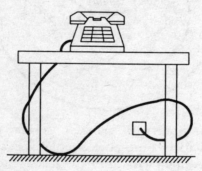

When we start to make quality a personal thing and decide to go in for a bit of self-improvement, particularly if you are the boss, it spreads like the plague. Eventually people stop looking for someone to blame for poor quality and take it upon themselves as individuals and in teams to make things better. Starting now, don't ever again walk past a poor quality happening without doing something about it.

Slice 17 Management Commitment

Commitment is simply deciding that you will do something, leadership is about doing it. Commitment cannot be faked, you either are, or you aren't committed. It describes an emotional state which is deeply rooted in the beliefs and conscience of people. Unfortunately, commitment to issues and people is often vague and half-hearted and compromise can result. This will not do for an effective TQM process.

The commitment of management to TQM cannot be delegated, you have to show your commitment by your actions. If you are a profitable organisation and then commit to TQM, the boss may see it as enough to commit the resources to TQM and delegate the rest. This will turn out to be a waste of money, because it will not work.

Quality must be a commitment of management, not just the job of the quality control department. Little or nothing will happen until management get involved. The people will automatically look for evidence that management is committed to the process of improvement.

Evidence of Management Commitment

- Management has developed a vision for the future of the organisation.
- The necessary resources have been committed in the form of time and money. In my experience, the people do not demand much money, particularly in the early stages. The greatest barrier is the availability of time.
- When solutions to problems are found, they should be promptly implemented. This is the gift of management. It's no good saying, 'Ah, yes, well remind me about that next week, I'm a bit busy with the 5-year plan at present'.
- Allowing the formation of problem solving teams and giving them the time and resources to deal with the problems. Does the boss attend problem-solving team meetings from time to time?

41

- Dismantling barriers between departments and listening to suggestions for improvement from anyone who cares to make them.
- Quality processes go through phases. After 1 to 2 years from the start, the process usually stalls. When this occurs, an evidence of management commitment is that the people see management revitalise the process.

TQM demands that organisations move away from 'Management by Control' to 'Management by commitment'. You don't have to be the immediate supervisor or boss of people to get things done. Effectively organised companies have managers who get their own way when they are right, and don't when they are not, irrespective of whether the people they are asking to change work directly for them or not.

 Politicians are utterly clear about words like commitment. They see 'commitment' as 'do in the future', 'concern' as 'do nothing', and 'participation' (Slice 18) as 'others to do'. The politician's interpretation of commitment will not do for organisations that need to improve their quality of goods and services.

Management of modern organisations means that all these key words are about appropriate ACTION.

Slice 18 Leadership

There's more to leadership than autocracy or democracy. As the One Minute Manager[5] says, 'you need to become a "situation" leader by "contracting" with your people about what kind of leadership they need through a "diagnostic" process of analysing their needs. You become "flexible" and manage them according to the contract you worked out with them.'

This is situational leadership and it needs practise because you don't have to *be* a situational leader, you have to learn to *behave* like one. Leadership is that quality in a person that induces others to follow. John Harvey-Jones called it 'Making things Happen'[11]. And remember, these people are both your customers and your suppliers and not just the people who work for you.

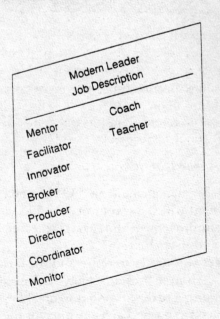

The leader cannot delegate leadership. If a subject is important, then the leader should be personally involved, seen and heard by his people. At times, this means getting your hands dirty with the details of what you are trying to accomplish.

The difference between the boss and his subordinates is that the boss doesn't get dirty as often as they do and when he does, he may as well arrange for the cameras to be on him.

Do not confuse leadership with mere authority, a tasty morsel that feeds upon itself for the self-gratification of the authoritarian.

18.1 Involvement and Participation

Participation by management in TQM is not enough. Only total involvement will show your people that you are committed to quality improvement. But what is the difference between involvement and participation?

Farmer Giles was about to retire and the farmyard animals decided to give him a present. They had no money so they formed a committee to discuss what to do. They finally agreed to give him bacon and eggs each morning for the rest of his life.

The hen was chair-person and as retirement day approached, she was talking in the committee about the award when the pig had second thoughts. She said, 'let's think about this some more, because Mrs. Hen, for you bacon and eggs is only participation, but for me it is total involvement'.

Get involved, get your hands dirty occasionally and demonstrate your commitment by your actions.

Slice 19 Styles of Leadership

When you are *leading* your quality process, be an educator, a communicator and the person with the Vision of where you are going and how you are going to get there and how you are going to measure your collective progress. There are many types of manager, which depends to some extent on their personality and the job they are doing. Michael Macoby[16] described them as *jungle fighter, company man,* and *gamesman.*

But what about the possible styles that can be adopted to be a 'situational leader', as the One Minute Manager asks. He describes these styles as 'Directing', 'Coaching', 'Supporting' and 'Delegating'. The type of leadership you use for each person you manage depends on the situation. It's neither democratic nor autocratic but simply practical. People are not equal, so don't believe you're at Animal Farm[12] where everybody is equal, but some are more equal than others. That's dishonest and lacks sensitivity.

You need to know what the overall goal is and the daily needs and guidance that each of your people requires. Some need one style of leadership and others need a different one. It all depends on the 'Potential' of the subordinate.

Some things can be managed, others delegated and yet others supervised. Do not delegate the responsibility for quality and at the same time don't confuse leadership with supervision. They are not the same thing at all because quality improvement is a management function, not a technical one.

19.1 Management Styles to Avoid

- Too many chiefs and not enough Indians.

It can be a catching habit, with more and more people telling fewer and fewer others what to do. Let's hope that eventually, they will become more enlightened and have fewer coxswains.

Four oarsmen and one cox is a great improvement, but it is by no means ideal because four out of five still can't see where they are going!

- Mushroom management: keep everybody in the dark and heap s*** on them often.
- Seagull management: fly in, s*** all over them and fly off again.
- Management by fear: do this or that or else you'll suffer.
- Management by exception.

These are management styles designed to 'control' people and are not as effective as styles designed to 'commit and empower'. When people are overly controlled, they are being encouraged to leave their brains at home before they set off for work.

Slice 20 Management By Walking About

Stew Leonard[14] hardly ever goes to his office during shop-opening hours. He is out on the floor of the dairy doing some Management by Walking About, (MBWA). Walt Disney did it, my local butcher does it and I hope you do it. It can transform your organisation.

Of course, if you haven't got any values and standards worth communicating to your people, then stay in your office and look for another job.

Tom Peters called MBWA, Management by Wandering Around, but this seems a bit aimless to me. However, whatever you call it, MBWA allows managers to remain in touch with Customers, Innovation and People, the three main areas necessary in the pursuit of total quality.

MBWA is probably the single best method of communication invented by man, with the possible exception of the grapevine (Slice 82).

While doing your MBWA, be sensitive and be one of the people. Richard Varey[20] called this style of management, ACUMEN. The dictionary defines acumen as 'Perceived skills', but Richard says it means:

Appreciation
Communication
Understanding
Motivation
Encouragement
Negotiation

Clever, ain't it? And obvious. Let's all DO IT!

20.1 From Sergeant to Parent

The perfect quality team leader is a coach, not a cox. The process of institutionalising quality improvement will require this change of management style to gradually happen. The sergeant major is used to having his way, and when he says 'die', they die.

Very wasteful and increasingly difficult to achieve. Impossible even. Running around telling everybody what to do can be great fun for those who lack respect for others and like driving the corporate fire engine, but it is unnecessary and counter-productive.

Coaching has to become the norm. The football coach does not participate in the match, she sits on the sideline, biting her nails in the expectations that her training will work during the play. When it does not, she goes back to the drawing board and rebuilds the team, not during play, but afterwards.

She and the players work in teams for the common good. Commitment to this principle is an essential ingredient for effective quality improvement.

When I was a child and my father threw me the beachball and I dropped it, he didn't shout, 'You stupid little sod, pick it up!'

He said, 'Don't worry, let's just try again.'

Through encouragement and coaching, management styles must change from sergeant major to caring parent.

The president of a major manufacturer of car components in the USA, spends 20 days per year in training workshops. He is not one of the students, he is *Helping To Do The Teaching*.

Slice 21 Motivation

You'll never motivate people by insisting that they do what you tell them. We cannot run our companies on military lines. 'Over the top,' says the officer. 'Buzz off' says the employee, 'there are bullets up there.'

It is very likely that whatever motivates you is the same as that which motivates others. If you are a manager, then strike a balance between 'satisfiers' and 'rewards'. Motivation comes from clarity of vision and leadership, which should not be confused with mere authority.

I attended a quality workshop some time ago where we did an exercise on motivation. We were invited to list 10 items which motivate us hourly/daily, and five items of a weekly/monthly and annual nature. Among the interesting motivators suggested were:

- achieving targets
- career promotion
- beating competitors
- recognition
- supporting the team
- fear of failure
- boredom

- self-esteem
- salary review
- personal appraisal
- ambition
- customer requests
- reprimand
- problem solving.

There were many more. However, the item that a few groups came up with was:

When did you last thank one of your people for a job well done? More important is the question, 'do you criticise more often than you praise?'

When people are motivated and encouraged to take their own decisions, management personnel have finally accepted that they no longer ask employees to leave their brains at home in the morning. There's an old adage that says:

Managers do the thinking
Supervisors do the talking
and Employees do the doing.

We must lay this foolishness in the ground, never to be dug up again.

Slice 22 TQM Process Ownership

If you buy a TQM model from a consultant (good idea), he will teach you the structure and philosophy, provide some manuals, slides and some ideas on how to start your ACTION process. If you ask him, he will come back repeatedly at great expense to you and teach you more of the obvious.

As soon as you have enough know-how and commitment to run your process yourself, consign the consultants to your Christmas card list and start to do it all by yourself.

If your TQM process is to be successful, you will have to own it yourself, along with all your colleagues and people until it is so ingrained as a way of life in your organisation that people say eventually, 'I wonder what happened to The Dizzock Consulting Partnership'.

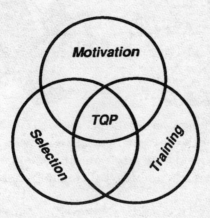

You select your people, empower them, motivate them, train them and you have TQP, Total Quality People.

22.1 People Empowerment

A cornerstone of TQM is the promotion of open-decision making. You empower the people to decide for themselves how to do things since they are the best qualified people to make decisions on their own behalf. But you can't do it without first giving them the skills they need by training and the information necessary to make meaningful and correct decisions.

Training and communication are the prerequisite essentials for the empowerment of the people.

The effect of empowering the people to decide for themselves is the release of the entrepreneurial spirit present in many of your people. They derive more job satisfaction, create a better working environment and leave their supervisors more able to plan and think.

John Akers of IBM said, 'Empowering our employees and inculcating a sense that everyone owns his or her piece of the business not only unleashes the talent and energy of our people, but flattens the organisation and reduces stifling bureaucracy.'

Slice 23 Drama, Enthusiasm and Sincerity

In all communications about TQM, be sincere, enthusiastic and occasionally dramatic. The Bard had the right idea when he said 'Friends, Romans, Countrymen, lend me your ears'. That's dramatic and is far more effective than saying 'Folks, I've got something I wanna tell ya'.

A course at drama school is not the answer, you are not learning to be an actor. However, if you have something important and worthwhile to say, there's great benefit to be had from shouting it from the roof-tops, in dramatic fashion, if you like.

The need for enthusiasm, sincerity and passion must come from inside, but you can refine it a little by learning good presentation skills. I once went on a presentation course where we were taught the principles of OTT, Over The Top. Children's television presenters are good at OTT. They are un-embarrassable people who do not mind raving. They can even turn 'I'm going to eat an ice-cream' into a drama. You don't have to go as far as a Children's TV presenter or Patrick Moore, the TV astronomer, but a bit of OTT is a good thing.

If you want to see how you look, make a video of yourself saying something. Before you have the benefit of seeing yourself making a presentation, you may feel you are an animated person, but you may appear to others to have the charisma of a dead cockroach.

Enthusiasm and sincerity, when shown and felt for real, can be very convincing characteristics in support of a valid argument or position. Being right is only of value when you can convince others to adopt your views. Some people can get away with blandness because of who they are. Someone once said of Geoffrey Howe:

> "....like being savaged by a dead sheep...."

Most of us are not like Geoffrey Howe, and need animation in some form to carry our day.

Even more slices, yes?

Slice 24 Quality on Fridays

If you ask all five billion people in the world if they are 'for quality', they will say 'yes'. Who but a fool doesn't want to improve? People do not resist the adoption of sensible principles. However, many managers and others will often say, 'I haven't the time at present' or 'I didn't realise it was my job', or 'I've always done it that way'. They see quality improvement as something to be done on Friday afternoons, time permitting. They treat it separately. Safety on Monday, management meetings on Wednesday, and Quality on Friday. Quality comes last.

'Hold on', you might say, 'we're not so bad, our products aren't perfect, but they are as good as our competitors'. OK, that's fine, so write yourself an advertising slogan that says:

That's a disastrous sales pitch. The fundamental problem is that they are treating TQM as a separate subject and saying 'quality gets *IN THE WAY* of what I am doing'. Better to say 'let quality be *THE WAY*' and make it an integral part of all business activities. You can also do it at home, quality that is.

24.1 Fire fighting

Stop driving the 'corporate-fire-engine'. All small boys, and some small girls wanted at some time in their childhood to be a fire engine driver, because it's fun. Of course, the feeling does not really go away; we tend not to state it when we get older, but it is still a fun idea.

So management has the authority to drive the corporate-fire-engine, but they will have to stop it and let someone else have a go while they spend some time on something infinitely more important:

> ## Improving your prevention techniques

I assume you've got some.

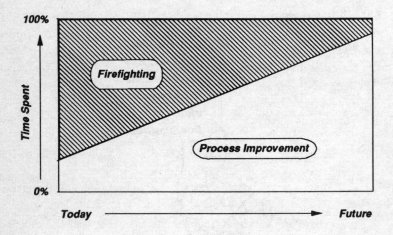

Eventually you have fewer fires to put out and you can get your fun from planning for crises instead of having to deal with their unexpected arrival.

If you really like putting out corporate fires so much that you can't do without it, you could always go into politics, but fire fighting is not an appropriate activity for Total Quality Companies.

Slice 25 Quality Improvement Barriers

There are endless reasons found for not getting on with a quality process.

The top 10 hit parade is[17]:

1. Management talks about quality, but they don't spend much time working on it.
2. Our quality effort involves less than half our people, and most of them are in production.
3. We've lost direction and momentum.
4. We don't have specific goals for quality as we do for other key areas like sales and production.
5. Performance evaluations still don't include accountability and rewards for quality improvement.
6. Our people don't seem to have fun working on quality improvement; it's just added work.
7. Everyone's trained in quality improvement, but they're not doing it.
8. Top management tells us quality is important, but they force schedules, ignore suggestions and don't listen to customers.
9. I haven't the time and we haven't the money.
10. We are already rather good, so we don't need it.

25.1 The Golden Rules

TQM seems to have a lot of rules about gold.

59

Joseph Juran (Slice 9), the Balkan born American guru said 'There's Gold in the Mine' to capture the notion that problems and mistakes should be viewed positively and be seen as treasures to be 'mined' because problems are opportunities for improvement.

When people know how to fix mistakes in such a way that they can be prevented from happening again, they are more likely to admit their mistakes.

The concept of 'Gold in the Mine' should not be confused with the 12 Golden Rules of Møller (Slice 11) or *the* Golden Rule that states that:

Whoever owns the gold makes the rules!

Slice 26 Departmental Cooperation or Rivalry?

It's obvious which one should be chosen, but how often is the correct one chosen?

26.1 Inter-departmental Rivalry

This is one of the biggest barriers to the success of a TQM process and one of the greatest challenges for the boss. However, when the barriers are broken down through training and the development of common goals (Vision, Slice 4), the benefits are enormous.

 The relationship between departments is often adversarial. Departmental managers wandering around like ageing lions marking the extremities of their territory and roaring to warn against encroachment by others.

What are they afraid of? Have they something to hide? It's usually mistakes, problems and other skeletons that their lack of cooperation with others has caused and buried in the first place.

The analysis of inputs and outputs from departments and processes ultimately produces good reasons for inter-departmental cooperation and a seamless interface between them for the benefit of all.

For a TQM process to succeed, these barriers to cooperation between departments must be gradually broken down by identifying customer/supplier relationships. Training and communication are the key to the removal of these barriers.

26.2 Cross Departmental Cooperation

After you have improved yourself by moving the telephone to the right position and keeping your desk tidy, etc., you can then set about improving your department. Since quality improvement is within the gift of departmental managers for their own people, subject to financial constraints, these departmental managers can make it happen. The real problems begin when you try to get another department to cooperate with you.

Question: Do you get what you want from other departments?

Answer: No, they don't meet my deadlines and they give me what they want and they don't seem to care about my department either.

Question: Do you give the other departments a detailed specification of what you want?

Answer: Er, yes, I suppose so.

I rest my case. Cross-departmental teams, or cross-functional teams have to develop characteristics that expedite communications and improve the efficiency of team members. When these cross-departmental teams work effectively, they allow the organisation to achieve more with fewer resources but they can only succeed if the departmental heads allow them to cross departmental boundaries.

You want it when? It happens all the time. Department A is supposed to provide the widget stock list (I never buy widgets, they are always faulty) to department B by Thursday. 'A' always has to ask 'B' on Friday for the list. 'I had to do something else', says B, not bothering to add, '. . . because it was more important to me'.

This attitude of mind does not, of course, extend to external customers, at least one hopes not. But internal customers are not as human as external customers. Department B is not populated by real people until we play cards in the canteen at lunch time. We can always let down other departments before we let down ourselves in our own department.

You want it when?

This failure to be on time is a Cost of Quality, subdivision, Cost of Internal Failure. (Slice 70).

Slice 27 Drive out Fear

When problems are treated like goldmines for improvement (Slice 25), there is less tendency to hide mistakes since the TQM process can be used to prevent the problems from happening again.

When managers and supervisors are unable to correct mistakes and then prevent them re-occurring, they look for someone to blame. Of course, it is hardly ever themselves, so someone lower down the hierarchy gets a regal rollicking for it. It is a common management failing to use:

Too much stick and not enough carrot.......

Looking for scapegoats makes people fleet of foot to the point where they can distance themselves from a problem more quickly than management can identify what and where the problem is. By the time the problem is out in the open, the goats have gone!

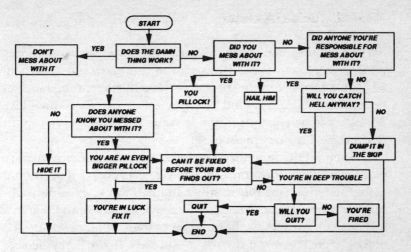

I heard of a pharmaceutical manufacturer who put the wrong labels on some drug bottles and got so worried about it that they instituted a policy of 'plant shut down' (Shigeo Shingo Slice 10) every time a serious problem occurred. They remained shut down until they had devised a method of preventing the problem happening again, and only then did they fix the problem. After that they restarted the plant. They had lots of shut-downs for a while, but gradually they prevented more and more problems and ran their operation more smoothly and efficiently.

You can only do this if you *drive out fear* and allow people to admit their mistakes so that the mistakes and not the people can be corrected.

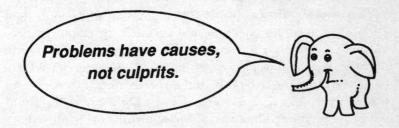

65

Slice 28 People Assets

Total Quality Management is mainly about hands-on people management. Much has been said in this book and elsewhere about management styles, commitment, participation, motivation, communication and all the other 'shuns' which are necessary to help people function well. You forget at your peril that people are your main asset.

As your TQM process takes hold, and tangible benefits are seen, more and more training will be necessary. International Computers Limited put in more than 10 days per annum off-the-job training, and Nissan UK provide more than 20 days.

The cynics often say about training that the more you do the more people leave and the more you have to do. They believe they will become their industry's training school. The facts suggest otherwise. International Computers Limited and Nissan aren't complaining. Their people are so well trained and motivated, that they could not bear the idea of working for an *inferior* competitor.

Do you promote from within? If not, then you probably have a higher turnover of people than companies who do promote from within. Of course, to fill jobs internally means you will need a personnel development plan. Do you know where the talent is to fill the retiring finance director's job, and have you alerted the person to the need to move up?

'We can't possibly promote him to the job, he's been
a site accountant for all these years, but he doesn't have
the breadth of experience to be the finance director.'

This is probably a rubbish statement, and if it is not, then you do not have an effective management development programme. You will go hire some whizz-kid from the outside, who may for all you know, only be brilliant at being interviewed. He or she may turn out to be OK, but no better than the people you passed over, and the new guy doesn't know anything about your organisation. Then the ultimate insult card is played:

Sorry we couldn't make you finance director, Percy, but Penelope was too good to miss. However, she doesn't know much about our company, so be a good chap, and train her, would you!!

No wonder people are under-motivated, disloyal and feel little pride in belonging. They are waiting for retirement or another job.

28.1 Good News – Bad News

TQM is not about only giving good news. It is not a guarantee that everything will always get better.

Economic cycles and unpredicted technological changes mean that at times business gets worse, not better. TQM, when implemented, can help you weather the storm. Tell your people the truth, even when the message is unpleasant.

People are always willing to believe the truth if they know you always tell it, good or bad. If you try to tell your people that *all London brothels display a blue lamp*, most of them know that's not true, and the few who go test the statement get into serious trouble.

Make your leadership statements and requirements do-able, sensible and authentic. Avoid being feeble. If you say 'Have you tried the famous echo in the reading room of the British Museum?', it is quite possible to go out and do it because it is DO-ABLE. However, it is not SENSIBLE and can lead to *even more* serious trouble.

Your quality message must be clear, concise, possible and authentic and must position Quality in the organisation in such a way that people give it the priority it deserves and feel positive about the goals which are set because the goals are positive and achievable.

Slice 29 The Shape of Success

Organisations that have succeeded in many of their quality improvement goals have common characteristics. You can recognise them everywhere. Marks & Spencer is a good example and another is the intensive care unit of a hospital. Their characteristics are as follows:

- They are customer driven, both inside and outside the organisation.
- They have the invariable attitude that the expectations of the customer come first.
- They respect *all* the people within the organisation and know that they each 'can', 'will' and 'want' to contribute to the improvement process.
- They place more emphasis on preventing mistakes than inspecting the errors out of the final product or service.
- They involve everyone in the decision making process.
- Their people know they are dependent on each other for improvement and they know that the success of the individual is a result of team success.

If your organisation is like this, then you've made it! If not, keep trying in small steps and often. Learn how to eat your elephant, slice by slice and bite by bite.

29.1 Self Gratification or otherwise

There is a danger that organisations say to themselves that they are successful. But is it really true?

TQM is a high profile activity led by the boss who puts a lot of time into making the process effective. This pulls a lot of other people along with it and large sections of the organisation can become quite obsessive about making the process succeed.

Under these circumstances, it is easy to see every little improvement as not only a reason to shout the success from the roof-tops, but also as a proof that the process has nearly achieved its goals. This is self gratification, particularly if you had unrealistic expectations about the shortness of the time needed to reach excellence. Be realistic, but avoid pessimism. Remember the emperor?

For large companies, it will take up to a decade to be able to say that 'our quality process has succeeded'.

A different kind of self gratification is to say in sales meetings, 'our profits (or turnover) have increased in the last quarter by 10%'. This does not prove that you are conforming to your customers' expectations. You may have increased prices to

70

achieve this goal, and if the customers are not happy about this, they may be beavering away at finding another supplier.

Beware of self-gratification, it can be deadly and your people may think you are out of touch with reality.

If you believe your primary business objective is to make a profit then you are confusing cause and effect. You are in business to serve your customers. When you have done that properly, you get the 'effect' of making a profit.

Without this view of 'cause and effect' about your business objectives, the concept that profit is self-gratification will not appeal to you.

Slice 30 Strategy and Quality

TQM can help you make the right strategic decisions about the future direction of your organisation. However, remember that strategy is about *doing the right things* and quality is about *doing things right*. Combine the two and you have *doing the right things right = success*.

You can have a faulty strategy and a perfect quality process with the result that you *do the wrong things perfectly*. The trick is to organise the organisation to behave in a way that is in the best interests of all concerned.

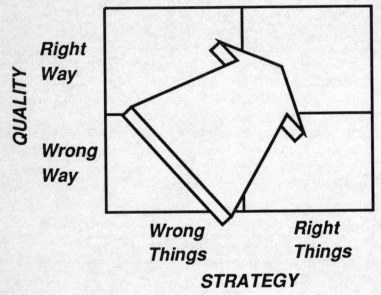

Keeping strategy and quality separate during the early stages of TQM implementation is probably a good thing, because it prevents people blaming the quality process for every little backward step that comes along. Ultimately, quality management and strategy are interlinked, indivisible and the same; but only after the quality culture becomes an integral part of how you run your business.

Peter Drucker had a different view of right and wrong, which is equally valid. He said:

72

Management is doing the right things.
Leadership is doing things right.

30.1 The Design Interface

Eventually, design, quality assurance and quality management are phases in your normal planning process and when you've reached *right first time* status, you will be able to look back and say things like:

> *We build quality in at the design stage.*
> *20 years ago, our management technique focused on costs,*
> *10 years ago our management focused on quality,*
> *and today management focuses on design.*

A further driving force for TQM implementation is the need for the *long term survival* of the Organisation and the need for a common culture that transcends country boundaries and allows you to be English in England, European in Europe, and a leader world wide.

When design of services, product, systems and procedures is the first concern of management after people issues, the organisation is really looking outward to find out what the expectations of customers really are. This is one of the best ways I know of preventing organisations becoming another

---

Clockwork Watch Industry

Slice 31 Organisation Behaviour

There are massive tomes on the theory of organisational structures and huge numbers of books on specific examples like the inner workings of IBM, ITT, ICI and I know not what.

The structure of an organisation, its hierarchical matrix and flow chart of responsibility, do not tell you how effective it is in the one area which matters. Does it conform to its customers' expectations? The accomplishment of high product and service quality is the result of effective organisational behaviour.

An organisation must clearly understand its purpose (Vision Statement, Slice 4) and then organise its behaviour accordingly. Otherwise, it may become 'Reggie Perrin Products (Unintentional) Ltd'.

As Frank Price[1] asks, 'Is a heap of bricks an organisation?' No, its a heap of bricks.

But if you build them into a structure they become organised bricks that can serve a useful purpose.

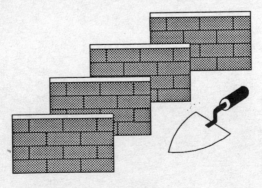

The same goes for people; they need an organisation to work in so that they can serve their purpose of *conforming to customers' expectations*. Companies must move from short-term to long-term goals. This will allow quality processes to succeed so that managers are no longer obsessed with short term profit rather than real improvement.

Message: Organise and behave first for the benefit of your customers, then for your employees and finally for the owners, in that order. (Slice 64).

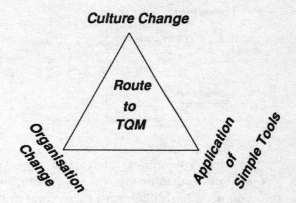

Slice 32 Organisation Charts

32.1 Company Organisation Chart

With this diagram, everybody knows where she stands and to whom she reports. This results inevitably in dotted lines, self-gratification or demotivation but you can't really do without it.

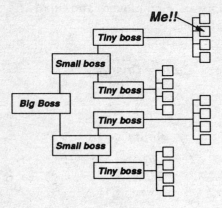

However, this diagram shows the reason why you are organising your organisation as you do. In reality, for large organisations, you need both diagrams, the second mitigating the 'turn-offs' of the first.

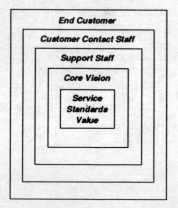

One of the better practitioners of 'practical' TQM is Whitbread Inns. They have organised their people into teams for the benefit of the external customer and portray their process as above. The cornerstones are Service, Standards and Value; that is what they expect to provide to their customers.

32.2 TQM Organisation Chart

The top-down organisation can be illustrated with the following type of diagram. The complexity of the organisation determines the complexity of the diagram.

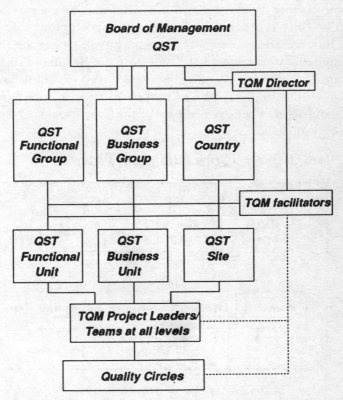

The important factor is that it should not be seen as a simple flow diagram, so arrows are replaced by lines to indicate the actions, up, down and sideways among the Quality Steering Teams (QST's) and Improvement Project Teams.

77

Slice 33 Implementing Process Analysis

A process is a series of activities strung together. Each activity has inputs and outputs. The inputs to each of the activities are transformed into outputs by doing tasks that add value to the inputs to produce useful outputs. When value is not added to the input, then the activity is useless because the output is not improved.[15]

The whole business process comprises Core Processes, Supporting Processes and Non-Routine business activities. The Core Process converts market opportunities into money and generates revenue. The Supporting processes are required to maintain the effectiveness of the Core Business Process and the Non-Routine Business Activities are 'one-off' occurrences or events that happen infrequently such as divestment or acquisition. They are not part of the Core Process or Supporting Processes.

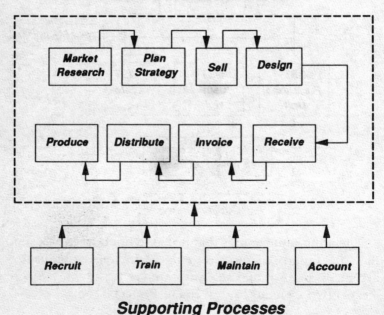

Core Business Process

Supporting Processes

78

However, the outputs from activities nearer the front of the Core Business Process must satisfy the requirements and expectations of internal customers if the whole process is to be effective.

Each of the activities is individually analysed and flow-charted to make up the Core Business Process. When the Core and Supporting processes are thoroughly understood, sources of improvement can be readily identified and worked on by project teams to ensure that planning and analysis are followed by DOING.

It is essential that much thought go into deciding what the various activities are and where an output from one becomes the input to another activity. A well-known car manufacturer in the United Kingdom used this system of implementing TQM and decided that their Core Process was as follows:

Core Business Process
(United Kingdom Auto Manufacturer)

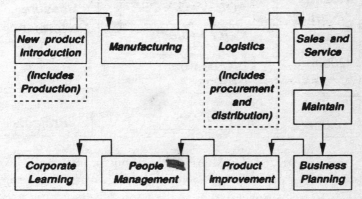

It is very different from the first diagram, but so long as the Core Process is clearly defined and understood by all the people, then the Process Analysis is effective.

79

Slice 34 Implementing the Integrated TQM Process

The implementation of the Integrated TQM Process should be as follows:

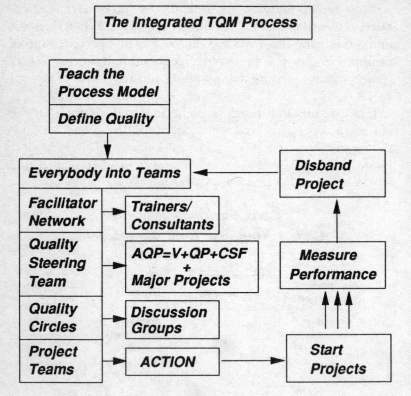

The Integrated TQM model is about teams at all levels, discussing, prioritising, selecting and running projects designed to improve quality in the name of conforming to both internal and external customers' expectations.

The process model concepts must first be taught to the whole of the organisation's people. These concepts must contain the fundamental beliefs, the cornerstones and keystones of the TQM philosophy and the reasons for organising, educating, communicating and caring about customer satisfaction.

The model must contain a suitable definition of quality and

know-how on the methods to be used for building a Vision Statement, Quality Policy, identifying Critical Success Factors and how to select projects.

The Annual Quality Plan (AQP) contains these data. A Vision Statement (V), Quality Policy (QP) and Critical Success Factors (CSF's). The projects which result from the deliberations of the QST's and Quality Circles should all be designed to make the CSF's, and in turn, the Vision, come true.

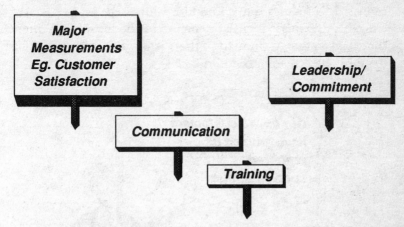

Many 'Related Actions' are necessary to 'lubricate' the process of improvement and to provide the skills and reasons for people to be enthusiastically involved in the 'Main Flow' of activities.

Even more slices!

Slice 35 Critical Success Factors

There are many areas of quality improvement that can be worked on, but some are more significant or critical than others. It is the job of the various QST's (Slice 39) to decide what these Critical Success Factors should be.

It is crazy to squander your quality improvement effort on projects related to the colour of the toilet paper when there are more critical issues that should be addressed.

CSF's are single focus statements in the form of a sentence that lead to the attainment of the Vision. For example, a CSF dealing with customers could be:

Our top 10 customers have granted us preferred supplier status

Notice that the statement is written in the present tense which means that it has become true. This then represents a goal to aim for and is more imperative. When it has been achieved, you change the statement from *10 customers* to, say, *15 customers*, which sets a new and higher goal.

Don't confuse Critical Success Factors with Critical Quality Costs. CSF's may be simple items such as better warehouse logistics to get the products out on time and may cost you almost nothing. Critical Quality Costs can be items such as energy efficiency being so poor that production costs are too high. In a competitive world you cannot pass these costs on to the customer, they hit your bottom line. Therefore, the customer may be already satisfied but the owners of the business are not.

35.1 Measuring Critical Success Factors

If a Critical Success Factor is not measurable or verifiable, then it is not a CSF. It should preferably be written so that the measurement of it is easy and straightforward. This is often not so simple. Therefore, verification of the CSF should be used. For example, the following Critical Success Factor is directly measurable.

CSF =
> **We have trained all our people in the principles of TQM**

You can directly measure it, and show the progress by drawing a graph of time against people trained for all to see. It does not say that they necessarily understand it or practise the principles of TQM. However, the CSF below is not directly measurable. It can only be verified.

CSF =
> **Our organisation is a welcome member of our local community**

It can be verified by the number and quality of newspaper articles, the number of environmental complaints from nearby residents, how easy it is to fill job vacancies, etc.

If a CSF contains a number, then even better.

CSF =
> **We have achieved >95% on-time delivery to our customers**

83

Slice 36 Quality Plan Deployment

The complete structure of decisions and activities are recorded in the Annual Quality Plan (Slice 37) and can be captured in one simple diagram based upon the Vision Statement (Slice 4) which sets the longer term goals, the Critical Success Factors (CSF, Slice 35) which define measurable shorter term goals and Projects which are designed to make the CSF's come true.

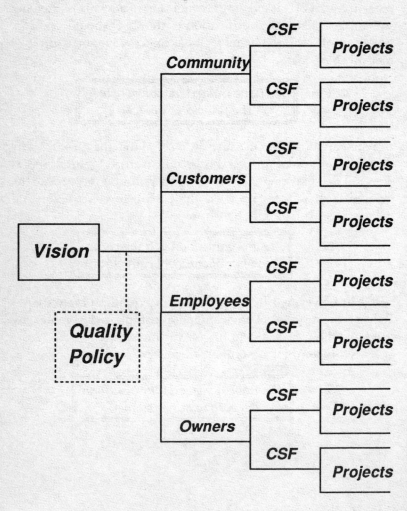

84

The whole process is guided by the Quality Policy (Slice 4) and the people make it happen by working in teams to achieve the goals. The Annual Plan (Slice 37) defines the decisions and activities for the coming planning period and the review dates of the projects show if the plan is on track.

The Road to Continuous Improvement

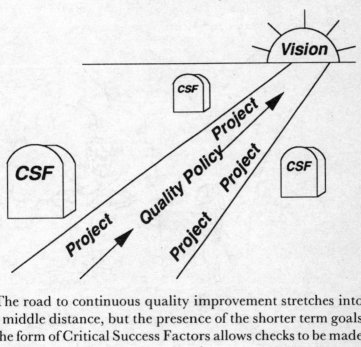

The road to continuous quality improvement stretches into the middle distance, but the presence of the shorter term goals in the form of Critical Success Factors allows checks to be made on progress. When changes to the plan are necessary, they can be made by paving the road with suitable projects to make the CSF's and visions come true.

Slice 37 Annual Planning

For those readers with a literary education, you will remember the story of Alice in Wonderland. Alice stood at the crossroad and wondered which way to go. In a tree was the Cheshire Cat. Alice asked the cat, 'Which way do I go?'.

The Cheshire cat said, 'Where do you want to go?'
Alice replied, 'I don't know'.
The cat said, 'Then both roads will take you there'.
This was one very bright cat!

Without an annual plan, you don't know where you are supposed to be going. Just like any other strategic planning activity, your TQM process needs an annual plan.

37.1 Annual Plan Contents

An annual plan for your quality improvement intentions is just like any other strategic or business plan. It contains in *quantitative* terms what you intend to do. The main sections will be as follows:

- **Vision Statement**

  This is developed by the Quality Steering Team and reviewed each year. If you said you would be 'a' leader some years ago, are you now 'the' leader? If so, then the Vision Statement needs changing.

- **Quality Policy**

  This is your guiding principle by which you will achieve your plan, and like the Vision Statement needs reviewing from time to time.

- **Critical Success Factors**

  These are short term 'visions' which should be measurable or verifiable. An important part of the plan is show how you are measuring these Critical Success Factors. Graphically, using the Quality Tools (Slice 48) is the best way, so that you and everybody else can see the progress. Set goals each year and show the progress from last year.

- **Major Projects List**

  You may well have hundreds of projects going on at each site at any one time. However, some of the projects are of greater significance than others. The Annual Quality Plan is the place to list and briefly describe your major projects and to record the expected impact they will have on the Critical Success Factors. Each project should be related to one or more Critical Success Factors.

  A factor of great importance about the Major Projects, is to show in the annual plan the Review or Completion dates for each of the projects. Without these dates, the situation is left open ended.

Slicing even better, yes?

Slice 38 Quality Teams

A cornerstone of TQM is the team building that leads to commitment to improvement. There are several types of Quality Improvement Teams.

Quality Steering Teams (Slice 39)
Quality Circles (Slice 40)
Facilitator Network (Slice 43)
Quality Improvement Project Teams (Slice 41)
Corrective Action Teams (Slice 42)

Membership in effective teams is very motivating because people have a feeling of *belonging* through their membership. They feel valuable. The teams have *Impact* because the talents and thinking of the team members have an effect on the choices and decisions made. The people *grow* when team members are empowered and encouraged to develop their own skills and abilities. Further, *meaning* is an essential for the effective motivation of teams. It implies that employees are doing something in which they and their supervisor believe.

38.1 Team Building

Individuals are important to any organisation. After all, each of us has our daily tasks to perform and nobody supervises every minute of our effort. That would be unproductive. However, in organisations involving many people, we work to a plan that requires us to take input from one person and output it to another.

To make the process successful, we need to recognise that we really operate in teams which can be a department, site, function, sales group or whatever. Building these teams requires common goals, a sense of belonging and ownership of the team process as a whole. One person cannot make meaningful quality improvement happen alone. By working in teams, which does not happen by chance, synergy and more job satisfaction develop. Teams are official and results orientated. Teams do most things better than individuals because the members stimulate each other; they possess a broader range of skills, and anyway, working in a team can be more *fun*.

The necessary skills for working in a team have to be learned. These include sensitivity to the group needs as a whole, analysing team collective problems, defining the goals and expected results, what to do when things go wrong, etc. Learning how to form and run a team effectively helps to overcome all those unpleasant human characteristics such as hostility, selfishness and cynicism. Teams make individuals better people.

Slice 39 Quality Steering Teams

QST's are composed of management and supervisory personnel with the responsibility to lead the quality process. They are formed by business units, sites, functional departments and countries.

QST's define the quality improvement goals for the coming planned period and organise the major projects. QST's are responsible for:

- The Annual Quality Plan.
- Defining the Vision Statement and Quality Policy.
- Defining the Critical Success Factors.
- Methods of measurement of Critical Success Factors and Major Projects.
- Training plans.
- Cost of Quality Measurement and reduction.
- Celebration events.
- The reward and recognition system.
- Major Project review dates.

These are the medium term tasks, but, in the shorter term, QST's must monitor and support the project teams assigned to specific improvement projects.

QST's provide the authority to *act*, define the projects and the key results needed to help the organisation achieve its Vision.

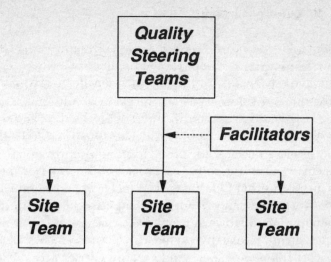

The operative word is *steer*. Don't run around deciding everything and treating your people like cannon fodder; let them decide as much as possible for themselves. This releases the commitment which most people feel anyway but which is often stifled by management who have a seemingly endless supply of humiliating barriers they erect in front of their people. These barriers are usually the result of management ignorance about how the operations and procedures of the organisation actually function.

NOTE: Quality issues are *all* the items of QST meeting agendas, but do you have quality improvement as an item at all other meetings? If not, why not? Have you got something to talk about that doesn't involve quality?

Slice 40 Quality Circles

Quality Circles are groups of 4–12 people from the same work area or from within a department, and often cross departmental boundaries. Their function is to identify local problems and recommend solutions. They meet on a voluntary and a regular basis to discuss, identify, investigate, analyse and solve their own work-related problems. The Quality Circle then present their solutions to problems and improvements to management when the solutions are not within their own gift.

The problems that Quality Circles tackle are not confined to quality topics, but can include anything associated with their work environment. However, topics such as pay and conditions of employment are usually excluded.

The cornerstones of successful Quality Circles are:

- Top management support.
- Operational management support and involvement.
- Voluntary participation of the members.
- Effective training of the leader and members.
- Shared work background.
- Solution oriented approach.
- Recognition of the Quality Circle's efforts.
- Have an agenda, minutes and rotating chairmanship.
- Keep to the time allowed for the meeting.
- Members should inform their bosses of meeting times.
- Make sure that Quality Circles are not hierarchical. If seniority plays any sort of part you'll find that the MD's secretary thinks she's too good to attend the regular secretaries Quality Forum.

Quality Circles are a marvellous system for developing a bottom-up approach to quality improvement and were invented by Ishikawa (Slice 10). Don't try them in isolation; make them an integral part of your quality process. Make them official, encouraged, attended and supported by management.

Not everybody wants to join immediately; many people see it

as another management ploy to exploit them. So don't force them to attend. You might get 25% in the first year, but the rest will come later.

There are more excuses for not going to Quality Circle meetings than for a bad golf shot. The favourite is 'I haven't got time'. Management should say, 'please go to your Quality Circle, because I exonerate you from any blame for the short-term harm that attending Quality Circle discussions might cause'.

Quality Circles help with the empowerment of the people.

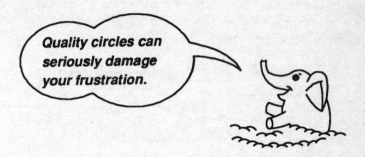

> Quality circles can seriously damage your frustration.

As well as the do's above, there are a few don'ts also:

- Don't let Quality Circles turn into 'sewing circles'.
- Don't let Quality Circles try to do the president's job.
- Don't let management interfere all the time. Attend, yes; run the Quality Circle, no.

When operated effectively, Quality Circles are a powerful force in any organisation. They are an important step along the way to empowering the people to use their talents and minds in your quest for quality improvement.

Great enthusiasm can build for Quality Circles. I have heard of many companies who found their people so enamoured with the system that the members gave their Quality Circles names, like, 'The Sparkies', 'The A Team', 'The Magnificent Seven' and 'The System Sizzlers'.

Slice 41 Quality Improvement Project Teams

The deliberations of QST's and Quality Circles result in the identification of areas requiring improvement. Quality Improvement Project Teams, (QIPT's) are composed of people with a stake in solving the problem (more job satisfaction) and are appointed by management to find and implement solutions to *specific* problems.

I have seen many projects that succeeded, but the team leader took all the decisions and did all the work. That's OK for a one person team, but is a failure if the project was supposed to be a team effort. Below is a typical flow chart of how project teams function and decide their actions.

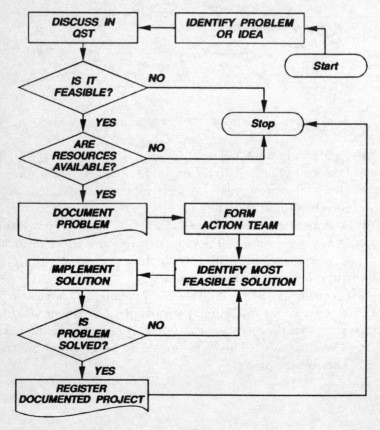

Slice 41.1 Corrective Action Teams

These teams are usually devoted to a specific short-term problem where the solution is known and can be fixed fairly quickly. They are set up by management with a clear, concise brief to correct the problem and are composed of people who are integrally involved with the problem and know all of its ins-and-outs.

However, Corrective Action Teams are wasted if they simply fix problems. Their real purpose is preventing the problem occurring again. A better name than Corrective Action Teams might be Preventive Action Teams or Problem Prevention Teams.

Slice 42 Project Team Requirements

- Project team leaders should be respected individuals with skills in project management.
- The Project Team needs direct authority from the QST.
- Make them cross-functional if you can. (Say, purchasing *and* production).
- Define the necessary tasks to be acted upon.
- Assign a responsible person for each task
- Prepare a chart showing when each task should be accomplished and make sure the team has sufficient resources. Not least of these resources will usually be the time to do the project.
- Make sure they are actively supported by an involved management.

Some of these requirements are the gift of management, but others should be decided by the project team itself. Make sure they are sufficiently trained and give them *status*. If management actively and visibly supports their project, the team will work harder at it and have a better chance of success.

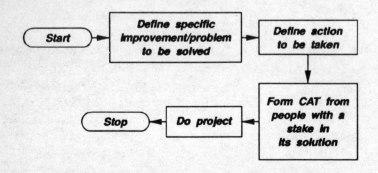

96

Slice 43   Facilitators and their Network

Facilitators are your 'agents of change' and help to ensure that positive changes do occur. Facilitators act as the conscience of the organisation and consultants to the process. Your network of facilitators must understand the quality improvement process, initiate and help the process of change from inside the organisation. For this they need training not only in the TQM process itself but also in areas such as team building, chairman-ship, problem solving, the tools of quality and the management of change.

Facilitators should be persons of standing in the organisation and slow to embarrass. Check their reputation carefully before selection. Choosing someone who the Chief Executive thinks is a good guy but most other people regard as a buffoon is no use at all.

Facilitating is about *Managing the Process.*
Facilitating is not about *Managing the Activity.*
Facilitators usually have a normal full time job and perform their role of facilitator in addition to this full time job by arranging secondment for periods of time too long to fit their normal work pattern. Being a facilitator is a privileged position and most facilitators are real enthusiasts for the quality improvement process.

The facilitator is the 'lubricant' for his department, site, business unit or country. The responsibility for the department is that of the department manager, and the facilitator is there to offer help and advice about the process methodology and possible training requirements.

Facilitators have an obligation to provide training and

97

advice to teams, to spread the quality message and to lead by example.

Most of us are used to either telling someone else what to do, or being told what to do. Facilitators must suppress their natural desire to lead and tell. They have a consultative role and possess no power other than that which the quality improvement process confers upon them.

The people who manage the change best are those who know the organisation best. The whole process of facilitator selection needs to be planned from the start, so discuss and decide and prepare a bar-chart (Gantt chart, Slice 50) which reflects your plan. Follow the changes according to the plan, be sensitive to activities which take longer than expected and follow-up the changes so that everyone can see management's priorities.

The process of choosing facilitators is rather simple.

I heard of a company where a manager said, '*If you can spare them, I don't want them*'.[27]. This neatly sums up the situation. Choose only your best people.

Slice 44 Project Generation

Good TQM means selecting and generating meaningful projects. They should be prioritised and evaluated based on the Organisation's Vision (Slice 4) and Critical Success Factors (Slice 35). The result is that everyone can see how his/her activities on project improvement teams fit into the overall goals of the organisation.

The steps of project generation could be as follows:

1. Quality Steering Team or Quality Circle defines a problem.
2. QST or Quality Circle prioritise the problem and define the scope of the project.
3. QST appoints a project leader, team members and project mentor who will be a more senior person in the organisation.
4. Guidelines and scope are communicated to the project team.
5. Review dates and expected date of completion are set.
6. The project is registered (see below).
7. The project is executed and monitored by the project mentor.
8. If the project succeeds, the success should be communicated to the appropriate people in order to give encouragement to them to be involved in project work of their own. If the project fails, examine why and re-define it if necessary.

44.1 Project Registration

All projects of significance, particularly those which cross country, site or departmental boundaries should be registered at each location. This makes them official and backed by management. Project registration also ensures that major projects are included in the Annual Quality Plan.

A non-bureaucratic procedure for project registration is required which is run by the secretary to the local QST.

Something along the lines of:

‹Site letter›/‹Year›/‹Project Number› will do. For example the *10*th project at site *C*leckhuddersfax for the year *1992* would be *C/92/10*.

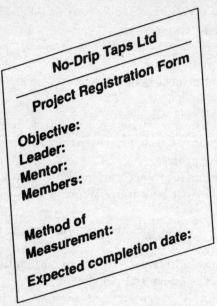

Devise a simple project registration form showing the name of the project, the objective, the methods of measurements, the names of team members, project leader and mentor, plus the required resources, review and completion dates. Make it simple enough for anybody to be able to complete it.

Slice 45 Project Organisation

Apply the *KISS* technique.

- **Keep It Sweet and Simple**

- Set priorities
- Define scope and title
- Write project definition
- Appoint project Leader
- Appoint members
- Agree check dates
- Do project
- Publicise success

Of course, management needs to measure not only the progress of the projects but also the results. It's no use publicising success if there is none. If a project does not work, guide it or disband it and start again.

Sometimes the project is succeeding but the project leader is doing all the work. Management has the responsibility to prevent this happening.

45.1 The Project Maze

An alternate way of viewing the route to effective project completion, is the Maze of TQM. Everybody, both management and the project team, are concerned to make the project a success, and this can be best accomplished by 'participative management'. But management must participate in the right way.

The project members simply 'go for it' but they must go into the maze from the right direction, the 'quality' (right way, wrong way). Management should concentrate on strategy (right things, wrong things). If either group blurs the interface between these issues, confusion and pitfalls result. In other words, management must allow the project team to do its job, and vice versa.

101

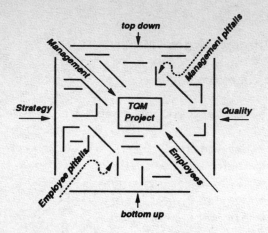

The successful completion of the project requires, patience, leadership and cooperation from all concerned.

45.2 Project Management

A cornerstone of TQM models is the running of projects to fix problems so that they do not happen again. Select project teams carefully so that the people fit well together. Most people like to be on a project team because it is a change from what they do on a day to day basis. However, projects need continual management support and encouragement so that they are successfully brought to a conclusion.

Projects should be properly defined, with a meaningful title, appropriate review dates, a project mentor who cares about getting the project completed and a goal that is possible. Failure to design projects properly can be disastrous.

The six stages of a poorly designed project.

1. Excitement/Euphoria
2. Disenchantment
3. Panic
4. Search for the guilty
5. Punishment of the innocent
6. Distinction for the uninvolved.

Well designed and run projects will rapidly push your TQM process forward.

Slice 46 Prevention versus Inspection

Many companies are organised in a way designed to inspect errors out of the system. This is followed by activities such as re-working, checking and repeating, which is expensive, frustrating and demotivating. It's a fire-fighting exercise and involves a hidden factory inspecting out and re-working mistakes.

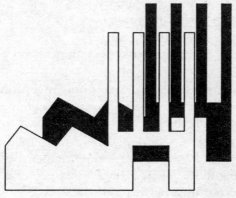

Inspection can require armies of inspectors, running about finding the errors and diverting management time away from running the business for the benefit of the customers.

If your error detection and 'do-it-again' system were perfect, then customers would be satisfied with your goods and services, but they will be either expensive or your bottom-line is inadequate. It makes more sense to satisfy the customer by using the technique of *prevention* which means identifying and fixing problems before they can turn into actual mistakes. Prevention techniques lead to more productivity, lower cost prices, a better market position and a healthier bottom-line.

Prevention is an attitude of mind and requires planning. It means you have to spend time on it, which becomes progressively more available as you stop fire-fighting. Prevention techniques require the measurement of activities to generate data which helps you identify where the problem areas are located. As Philip Crosby says 'Quality is Free'.

Slice 47 What Quality Means

There's a big difference between what quality '*is*' and what quality '*means*'. When you say quality '*is*' you are giving your definition of quality and this is unchangeable. When you say quality '*means*', it is one of a multiplicity of practical interpretations of your definition of quality. So quality can *mean:*

- being polite on the telephone.
- getting things 'right first time' every time.
- aiming for zero defects.
- being flexible and responsive to change.
- delivering on time and in full.
- tackling the source, not the symptoms of a problem.
- admitting your most valuable resource is your people.
- having a cost effective, workable quality system.
- measuring the progress of quality improvement.
- solving problems by discussion not conflict.
- never having to say, 'I'm sorry'.
- improving your own performance.
- cooperating and not confronting.

Quality does not mean just making things for the top of the market. Quality means providing products and services that do what they are supposed to do.

Quality is important for only two reasons – you care about your customers and the survival of your organisation. If you don't care, then don't waste money and effort on quality improvement.

Quality is never an accident, but the result of intelligent effort.
John Young

Slice 48 Quality Improvement Tools

These do not come in a box from a DIY shop and do not include a hammer.

If the only tool you possess is a hammer.......

The quality improvement and measurement tools are sensitive instruments and used to help identify issues, problems and sources of improvement as well as to represent the solution to a problem or to show the plan to be used to tackle the problem. There are many tools used in effective quality processes, but many are well beyond the scope of this book. However, the main tools are shown below and can help considerably with your intention to improve your business.

- Flow Charts
- Cause and Effect Diagram
- Scatter Diagrams
- Functional Analysis
- Failure Mode Effect Analysis
- Nominal Group Technique
- Simple Statistical Process Control

- Gantt Charts
- Pareto Analysis
- Line Diagrams
- Control Charts
- Histograms
- Brainstorming

Let's not forget common sense and general knowledge, although in my experience common sense is rather uncommon and general knowledge is hardly ever general!

When these tools are used, they look like the diagrams below:

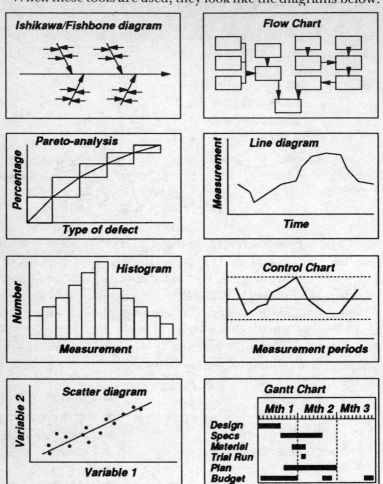

To illustrate the use of most of these quality measurement and problem solving tools, let's look at the baking of some loaves of bread.

Slice 49 The Baker's Dough

Bakers make bread from flour, water, yeast and, no doubt, a few other things like air. When the dough has 'risen', it is cut into pieces so that it can be baked into bread. The size of the lumps needs to be carefully controlled.

The easiest way to find out how 'consistent' the lumps of dough are is to weigh them. Our master baker knows that the correct weight of the 'perfect' lump of dough is 495 grams.

He wants to find out if the automatic dough cutting machine is accurate enough to meet the size specification of the finished loaf of bread. So he allowed the automatic dough cutting machine to do its job and then accurately weighed (grams) the lumps on a calibrated scale with the following results for 50 lumps of dough.

496	499	491	488	484
491	481	491	495	494
494	487	492	487	511
506	496	496	494	496
489	496	499	495	488
489	496	499	495	488
494	486	499	503	496
494	480	496	490	496
495	496	492	492	503
497	496	488	511	492

He wrote down the consecutive values in a table. Unfortunately, putting the values into this table, gives no clear picture but at least he has recorded the data.

The baker rearranged the 50 values from the table into ascending order and placed them in a second table.

107

480	489	494	496	497
481	489	494	496	499
484	490	494	496	499
486	491	494	496	499
487	491	494	496	499
487	491	495	496	503
488	492	495	496	503
488	492	495	496	506
488	492	495	496	511
488	492	496	496	511

The data already looks better, but further improvements are possible (see Slice 53).

Slice 50 The Baker's Gantt Chart

Our Master Baker realised that to conduct his investigation properly, he needed to do things in the right order, so he prepared for himself a time chart, usually called a Gantt chart.

Checkpoints for Baking Experiments

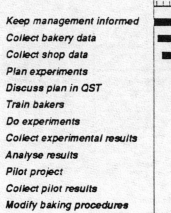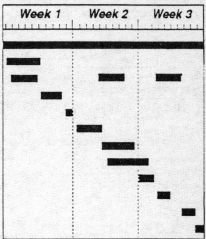

A Gantt chart can be used as an aid in the planning of work. Primarily, it shows the relationship of activities against time and highlights where the time planning has gone awry. Further, a Gantt chart shows where activities need to be started and finished in relation to other activities.

A Gantt chart is a time based chart showing the start and end points of various time based tasks.

Slice 51 Flow Chart

To ensure that the team of people assembled to address the baker's problems are fully involved and can make their maximum contribution, it is necessary for them to have a common view of how the process of baking bread really works.

They constructed a visual representation of the flow of the process in the form of a flow chart.

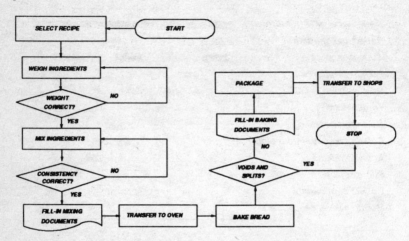

A flow chart is a pictorial representation of the steps or activities that constitute a process. They are often used to show the structure of an organisation or used to show the flow of computer programmes.

Different shaped boxes represent different types of issue such as 'document', 'decision', 'termination' or 'choices'. 'Flow lines' are inserted between the boxes to show the direction of the flow.

Slice 52 Cause and Effect Diagram

This is also known as a Fishbone Diagram or Ishikawa Diagram after its inventor (Slice 10). This quality measurement tool is a great help in brainstorming sessions (Slice 61) because it helps to display the possible causes of a specific problem or condition.

Put the goal or idea at the head of the fish and divide the contributing factors to the achievement of the goal into categories such as the 4M's, Men, Machines, Materials and Methods. There are several other M's you may care to consider as titles, such as Maintenance, Measurement, Markets and Money. However, the four M's in the diagram are the classical ones and sufficient for most purposes of thinking about issues to be considered.

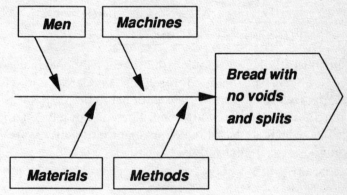

The contributing factors that affect each of the 4M's can then be filled in by the problem solving team. The ribs fit to the backbone and sub-ribs to the ribs and so on until you are satisfied you have captured all the issues.

Before the Master Baker's team went on to try to solve the problems they had, they decided to list all the issues. They used a fishbone diagram for this, because it helped to show where the relationships exist between one issue and another. It was also a very stimulating way of getting the ideas to flow from people. The use of a fishbone diagram in conjunction with the Nominal

111

Group Technique (Slice 61) can be a very effective way to identify possible solutions to problems.

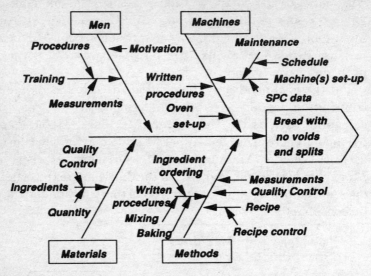

The finished diagrams look rather like a fishbone, hence the name, and can be very comprehensive. Cause and effect diagrams are useful to show the relationship between one issue or contributing factor and another. They do not tell you about priorities, which are best tackled using other quality representation and measurement tools.

Slice 53 The Baker's Tally Sheet

From Slice 49, let's divide the values into ranges from the lowest to the highest values in 'classes' of 4 grams. We then tally the frequency of the values per 'class'.

The result is a Tally-Sheet.

Classes	Mid point	Talley	No. in Class
480-<484	482	//	2
484-<488	486	////	4
488-<492	490	𝖧𝖧𝖪 𝖧𝖧𝖪	10
492-<496	494	𝖧𝖧𝖪 𝖧𝖧𝖪 ///	13
496-<500	498	𝖧𝖧𝖪 𝖧𝖧𝖪 𝖧𝖧𝖪 /	16
500-<504	502	//	2
504-<508	506	/	1
508-<512	510	//	2
			50

The sheet allows us to 'tally-up' where the clusters of similar values are located to give a more meaningful shape to the data. Even further improvements (or different ways of looking at the data) can be obtained by constructing a histogram. (Slice 55).

Slice 54 The Baker's Line Diagram

A line diagram simply plots variables against two axes to see the shape of the curve. From the table on Slice 49, our master baker wants to see the relationship between the weight of his lumps of dough and the consecutive lumps weighed because it gives him a pictorial representation:

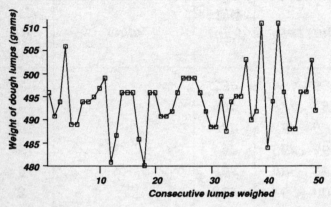

This proved nothing other than that there was a wide variation of weight and that the process of weighing consecutive lumps of dough did not show any meaningful pattern.

But suppose the shape had been as follows:

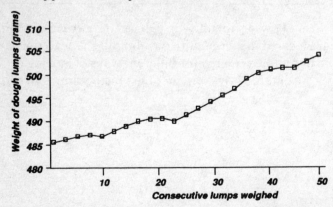

The weight would have been rising with consecutive lumps weighed. It would have allowed a completely different

114

conclusion to be drawn. This was not the case; the relationship between consecutive lumps weighed and the weight of the lumps showed a random relationship.

Slice 55 The Baker's Histogram

Let's use the tally-sheet to build a histogram. The horizontal axis represents the mid-point of the 'classes' of data and the vertical axis the number of lumps of dough in the 'class'. Patterns of data are now easier to see in this pictorial representation of the data, which is more meaningful than the numbers themselves.

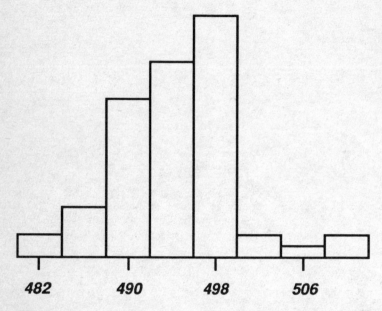

Histograms show different shapes and can indicate a probable cause for the deviation from the most frequent shape (= normal).

The above shape shows a 'skewed' relationship for the data.

55.1 Histogram Shapes

Histograms are used to display and identify the type of distribution of data by graphing the number of units in each cell or class.

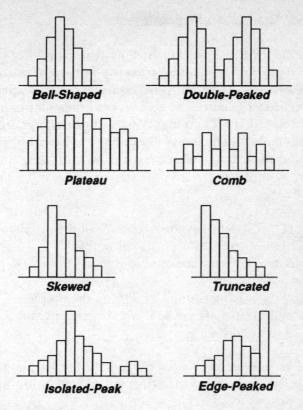

Bell-Shaped

Double-Peaked

Plateau

Comb

Skewed

Truncated

Isolated-Peak

Edge-Peaked

Different shapes of histogram, provide an insight into the value of the data. A normal or bell-shaped histogram is the most common shape. A double-peaked histogram may indicate that multiple 'populations' have been mixed together which means that two sets of data which were thought to be one have been mixed together. Histograms can indicate the reasons why processes are incapable of holding the required tolerances.

Slice 56 The Pareto Principle

The Pareto Principle was invented by Ishikawa (Slice 10) and is used to divide the 'vital few' from the 'important many'. It is particularly useful where it is necessary to decide on priorities for say, Critical Quality Costs. There is little point in fighting the battle where it isn't raging. Working on an aspect of quality problems that is small and of low impact, is obviously going to bear less fruit than one which has a greater impact.

A few examples of Pareto type statements serve to illustrate the point.

- 80% of quality costs come from 20% of the problems.
- 80% of sales go to 20% of the customers.
- 80% of the performance of people comes from 20% of their activities.
- 80% of the talking is done by 20% of the people.
- 85% of problems are caused by management and 15% are caused by subordinates.

The Pareto Principle is used to catch the big fish and to leave the little fish in the pond for attention at some future time.

56.1 The Baker's Pareto Table

Apart from getting the weight wrong, our master baker is also having trouble with a few other things.

He listed all his quality defect troubles in a table and counted the number of times that the defect occurred and then rearranged the data in order of frequency into a Pareto Table.

This table was then used to construct the Baker's Pareto Diagram.

56.2 The Baker's Pareto Diagram

A Pareto diagram is a method of showing the causes of defects which are the most important. It divides the vital few from the

Name of Defect	Number of Occurrences	Cumulative Number
Wrong Weight	128	128
Wrong Shape	91	128+91=219
Too Crusty	36	219+36=255
Underdone	23	255+23=278
Voids	15	278+15=293
Splits	9	293+9=302
Other	12	302+12=314
Total	314	314

important many. The data from the Pareto Table shown above was used to construct this Pareto Diagram using the Pareto Principle.

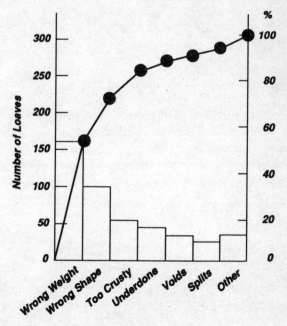

This representation of the data is yet another method of 'viewing a picture' of the data and can help in predicting the effectiveness of improvements and enable an understanding of problems and their seriousness at a glance.

Slice 57 The Baker's Scatter Diagram

Since our master baker so far found no relationship between weight of the lumps and the consecutive batches, he went looking for other variables that might explain the variations. He made a table of the weight of dough lumps against the incidence of different defect types. The table relating to the number of voids and splits is shown below.

Wt. (g)	No. Voids / splits	Wt. (g)	No. Voids / splits	Wt. (g)	No. Voids / splits	Wt. (g)	No. Voids / splits	Wt. (g)	No. Voids / splits
480	10	489	6	494	2	496	3	497	5
481	9	489	5	494	1	496	3	499	6
484	8	490	5	494	3	496	2	499	7
486	8	491	5	494	2	496	3	499	6
487	8	491	5	494	2	496	2	499	7
487	7	491	4	495	0	496	4	503	8
488	7	492	3	495	1	496	3	503	7
488	7	492	4	495	0	496	3	506	8
488	6	492	3	495	1	496	3	511	9
488	6	492	4	496	2	496	3	511	10

Then he plotted the various different defects in the baked bread against the weight of the lumps of dough and discovered that when the dough had 'voids' or 'splits', the dough weight had deviated the most from his aim of 495 grams. He discovered this from a scatter diagram, which is shown over.

121

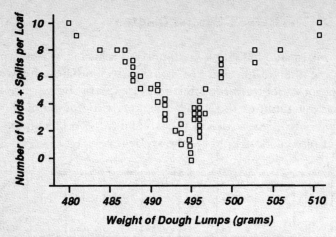

This proved to be a problem associated with the mixing of the dough that could not have been eliminated by increasing the accuracy of the automatic dough cutting machine.

Scatter diagrams show the relationship between two variables and each point represents a pair of variables.

Slice 58 The Baker's Control Chart

After a great deal of effort our master baker began to really get his act together and discovered that the weight of dough lumps had little to do with the accuracy of the dough cutting machine, but the weight did alert him to all sorts of other problems related to potential defects in the baked bread. He was able to control his process using the weight of dough lumps. He plotted his weights on a control chart.

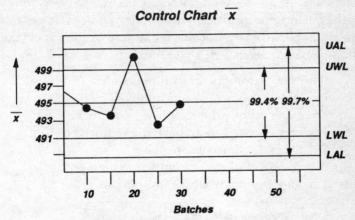

Control Chart x̄

The dough lump weight accuracy improved to such an extent that he could use the average of five lumps for plotting purposes. This is represented as $\bar{x}$ (pronounced, bar *x*). UAL means Upper Action Limit, UWL means Upper Warning Limit, LAL means Lower Action Limit and LWL means Lower Warning Limit.

Statistical analysis shows for a process under control, that 95.4% of the values are between the Warning Limits and 99.7% of the values are between the Action Limits.

123

Slice 59 Activity Analyses

Functional Analysis and Failure Mode and Effect Analysis are two of the many types of activity analysis that illustrate the point that paper work tasks can be analysed as a process just as you would analyse a manufacturing process.

59.1 Functional Analysis

Functional Analysis is a process for identifying quality improvement opportunities within a department or organisation, and is particularly suitable for administrative operations.
  Functional Analysis helps you find:

(1) Who the customers and suppliers are.
(2) The expectations of the customers.
(3) The expectations the suppliers must meet.
(4) The tasks needed to achieve the required output.
(5) The necessary measurements.
(6) Where expectations are not being met.
(7) The improvements which are possible.

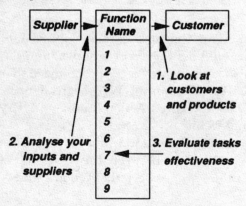

The steps necessary to conduct a Functional Analysis are shown in the diagram. After the various tasks of the function have been identified, they are categorised into the following work-types. This aids the search for areas of improvement.

- *R*equired-work
- *P*revention-work
- *A*ppraisal-work
- *F*ailure-work

When conducting a Functional Analysis ensure that it really is a function and not a process. If it is a process, then it should be broken down into its various functions and each one treated separately. Examples of Functional Analysis are:

'booking and order',

'receiving a complaint',

'garotting a donkey',

etc.

59.2 *Failure Mode and Effect Analysis*

Failure Mode and Effect Analysis (FMEA) is an analytical method of predicting what can go wrong with a product or service. The system of using FMEA breaks down the predicted failures into their root causes and 'grades' the risks involved. Unacceptable risk levels are selected for corrective action and the final risk level reduced to acceptable proportions[19].

FMEA is divided into two categories, Design FMEA and Process FMEA. Both require a team approach in order to analyse them. A specialised form is used to record the findings of the team of analysts. The team members start by defining customer expectations by asking the customer what he expects and then drive the production or service process into failure mode by dreaming up all the things which could go wrong and deprive the customer of his just expectations. After prioritising the possible failures, they are systematically prevented from happening.

The failure modes are recorded on the specialised form in terms of severity, effect, frequency and detection in order to obtain Risk Priority Numbers.

This team-based analysis is conducted for both Design FMEA and Process FMEA.

Although this may seem to be a formidable task, it has been observed by users of this type of analysis, that a little practise produces rapid results and priorities. The result is better products and services because defects are eliminated at the design stage, a condition more acceptable to the customer and more profitable to the supplier.

Slice 60 Statistical Process Control

Statistical Process Control (SPC), is a fancy term for analysing how your business processes are performing using numbers, diagrams and pictures. SPC does not have to be confined to production processes alone; SPC can be used to understand the workings of any activity from which numbers can be derived by measurement. SPC helps to:
(1) Evaluate long term the process variables (pattern recognition).
(2) Start short term actions on out of control situations.

Some people see SPC as the starting point of TQM. Personally, I view it as one of the Quality Tools used to help quantify the progress of improvement of the TQM process as a whole.

At its simplest level, SPC is illustrated by the *Average*.

The numbers 495, 496, 497, 498, 499 and 500 have an average of 497.5 and this is represented as $\bar{x}$ which is calculated from:

$$\bar{x} = \frac{\text{Sum of values}}{\text{Number of values}}$$

The average can be used to construct control charts (Slice 58). After that, SPC gets more and more complicated and is a subject of most interest to the experts. However, the result of SPC can be presented using a variety of the quality tools described elsewhere in this book, and the method of constructing the various representations should be taught to process operators so that they can do their own process control. Huge volumes of extremely boring but invaluable data and know-how have been written on SPC. Nobody seems to have written the 'idiots guide to SPC'.

Slice 61 Nominal Group Technique

The Nominal Group Technique is a simple technique, similar to brainstorming, for stimulating ideas, points, issues or solutions, among groups of 4-10 people and then taking a vote about the ideas with the highest priority in the opinion of the group.

1. Participants *silently* write their individual list of ideas.
2. They offer in rotation one idea each for recording on a flip-chart until all ideas are written down (no discussion yet).
3. The ideas are then discussed and similar/related ones grouped together as one idea with words which capture the group of ideas. The listed ideas from which the grouped idea came are then deleted in order to avoid duplication.
4. Each participant votes on the ideas. Say, 7 points for the best idea, 6 for the second best idea and so on down to one vote for the seventh best idea. The rest of the ideas do not get a vote from that participant.
5. Add up the individual votes to prioritise the list.

The Nominal Group Technique stops the boss saying, 'It's only a suggestion, but let's not forget who's suggesting it'.

With the Nominal Group Technique, silly or impractical ideas cannot be rammed down the throats of others because they simply get voted out. The Nominal Group Technique is a good way to stimulate the brain cells, hence the often used name, brainstorming.

A few less slices, no?

Slice 62 The Cellular Kitchen

There are a large number of *small* quality improvement tools such as the cause-and-effect-diagram and flow charts, etc. In addition to the small tools, there are the *system* tools, such as Just-in-Time, Materials Requirement Planning (MRP), Single Minute Exchange of Die (SMED), etc.

Many of these systems are clouded in mystery for most of us, but in reality, they grew out of common sense and the principle of simplicity. I shall illustrate some of these systems using the concept of a household kitchen, which can be a marvel of good lines, pleasing appearance and all the labour saving gadgets in the right place. A triumph of modern design. In the story that follows, the system or concept, of which the item is an example, is shown in *italics*.

The best designed kitchens (*Industrial Engineering*) work in an anti-clockwise direction, the most comfortable direction for people who are right handed, which is most of us.

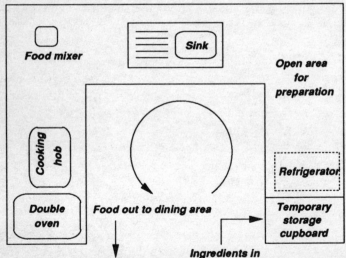

On the right we have the storage cupboards and refrigerator from which the ingredients are taken and prepared on the open work area. The sink is not part of the main process but is used so often that it is placed at the centre of the process. If you turn left at the sink you come to the oven and hob and a bit further left is the dining area where we eat our 'vittles'.

It may seem rather obvious that you don't put the oven in the loft and the food mixer in the cellar, but very often in factories, the layout is all wrong because the processes have changed and evolved over the years but nobody changed the layout. A kitchen is an example of *Cellular Manufacturing* where equipment layout is an essential part of planning and running a process in order to achieve *Product Flow*.

In the course of making lunch, I shall indulge in *Multi-process Handling* by having the hob, oven and mixer all running at the same time. In traditional manufacturing, it is likely that we would have a 'one-man-one-machine' situation, which can be labour intensive and inefficient. No modern kitchen would run on this basis. *Multi-process handling* reduces the labour time needed by having the various parts of the process close together.

Multi-process handling reduces the number of people needed and means that I can make the lunch all on my own while my wife goes to the pub. Otherwise, neither of us would have any fun!

The composition of the meal is decided and a list prepared of the ingredients and quantities necessary (*Materials Requirement Planning*), which in turn is a part of *Total Manufacturing Management*. The ingredients for the Sunday Lunch then have to be bought. All of them can be bought from the local supermarket, at convenient times, from suitably laid out displays and can be paid for using a credit card. The supplier has anticipated accurately our needs as a customer. This represents an example of *Partnership Sourcing*; my wife and I are in partnership with the supermarket.

The ingredients are stored in the temporary storage cupboard and refrigerator in time for making the Sunday Lunch. The meal is for 4 people and an appropriate sized piece of beef has been purchased. We don't buy a whole cow (*Nonstock Production*).

Slice 63 The Sunday Lunch

You'd be amazed how many bits and pieces of ingredients and equipment are necessary to make a Sunday Lunch. We have decided to have roast beef, Yorkshire pudding, carrots and crusty bread. I hear you say, 'I don't like the menu'. Then I suggest you don't come to lunch!

The time to start the cooking of each part of our Sunday Lunch is planned according to how long it will take to cook each one. There is little point in putting the carrots on at the same time as the roast beef. If you do, you get burned or mushy carrots. Each part of the meal needs to be ready at the same time or *Just-in-Time* and available in the right quantities to avoid the need for storage. What do you do with a whole cow, roasted or not? I suppose we could buy an industrial freezer and leave the car on the driveway, but it wouldn't be very efficient.

While the roast is cooking, I embark on a bit of *Multi-process Handling* by cutting up the vegetables on the clear area next to the refrigerator.

I now mix the Yorkshire Pudding (the ingredients are secret and controversial), and for this the food mixer fitted with a whisk is needed. I also need the food mixer fitted with a dough hook to make the bread. It's cheaper to have one mixer and several attachments than a separate mixer for each attachment, so easy change-over of one attachment for another is desirable. This is achieved with simple 'push-fit' attachments and is an example of *Quick Changeover*, or *SMED*, *Single Minute Exchange of Die*. Who wants a food mixer where the whisks have to be changed by unscrewing them with a spanner.

The beater whisk is actually two whisks that overlap when in action. There is no need to look for 'left' and 'right' whisks, they are interchangeable. If it was necessary to use left and right whisks, we could have Yorkshire Pudding mix all over the kitchen. The mistake of putting the whisks in the wrong side of the mixer is eliminated by making them interchangeable. It is good design, it cannot be done wrongly, it is the activity of mistake-proofing, it is *Poka Yoke*.

132

Washing-up can be done *In-process*, because the sink is in a handy place. In other words, you do it when you have time but it does not constitute an integral part of the main process of cooking the Sunday Lunch. However, if you had to go down the garden to do the washing up, it would all be left until after the meal had been eaten and could not be done *In-process*.

I know that the bread and the beef need to go into the ovens after they had warmed up to the right temperature. So, to ensure that the bread and beef are both ready at the same time, it is necessary to turn on the electricity to the ovens about 15-minutes before the bread or beef are due to go in. So the *Set-up Time* for each oven is about 15 minutes and for both kitchens and industrial operations, *Set-up Times* should be kept to a minimum. All of this timing information is carried in my mental *Gantt Chart* which if I had drawn it out on paper would have looked as follows.

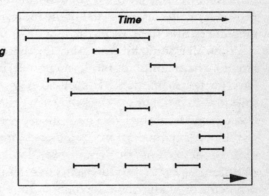

From the weight of the beef, and the temperature of the oven and my handy cooking time chart, I know how long was needed to cook the meat to the family's taste. This provides a guide only. The definitive time of roasting is determined from the internal meat temperature. I stick in a meat thermometer, and from time to time I check to see what it reads. If the meat thermometer had been connected to the electricity supply and turned off the oven when the internal meat temperature was correct, then this would have been an example of *Jidoka*, 'automation with a human touch'.

I keep checking the water level in the carrots (*Visual Control Systems*) to make sure they don't boil dry and finally, I put the food on the table and the family eats it. Unlike the Ancient Romans, we do not have an official taster, we stick it straight in our mouths and go 'yum-yum'. We do not exercise any quality control by inspection (*Zero Quality Control*). At the end of the meal there is nothing left over, no waste and nothing to store. The whole process is efficient and meets the customers' expectations.

We have made only one lunch at once (*Reduced Batch Size*), the *Cycle Time* has been minimised by making it *Just-in-time* to eat and the *Lead-time* on the supply of ingredients was minimised by collecting them from the supermarket on Saturday. We applied the common sense of the *Just-in-Time* principle which says 'when you have made what is needed, stop production and save the cost of the materials, wear and tear on machinery and the cost of the labour to produce it.'

When all is said and done, the effective operation of a modern kitchen is a triumph of modern engineering and design and is like 'poetry in motion'. It's all so obvious, and most of the solutions to problems in the kitchen are ridiculously simple, but it took us thousands of years to evolve efficient systems of cooking. Some modern practitioners of manufacturing process improvement, one of whom was Shigeo Shingo, applied common sense to produce effective simple solutions to the problems of modern mass production of high quality goods.

63.1 Just-in-Time

In the narrow sense, JIT is a process where goods, components, parts or documents are at the necessary place just at the necessary time. In the broader sense, JIT means moving materials to the correct and *useful* place, and takes place only at a time when the movement needs to take place.

A cynical view of JIT is that it is a clever method of getting suppliers to pay for your inventory costs and keep your working capital down.

However, for many companies, particularly those in partnership with their customers (Slice 92), JIT represents an important part of quality management. Toyota were asked about JIT. 'What happens if the truck bringing the parts breaks down?'. The Toyota man said, 'we stop production until the parts arrive'. They will not compromise on quality.

Too early means that the goods cannot be accommodated, and is just as bad as the goods arriving too late which causes the process to stop. It's got to be Just-in-Time.

The heart of Just-in-Time work is *Change-over Methods* and *Work-flow*, which makes the whole process effective. To do this, a large number of issues must be addressed using many different systems including, *One-piece Flow*, *Cell Technology Manufacturing*, *Multi-process Handling*, *Quick Change-overs*, *Visual Control Systems*, *Kanban and Andon*, etc. In addition, a good application of simplicity and common sense is highly beneficial.

Slice 64 CCEO Priority

This does not mean Ch-Chief Executive Officer, it means:
Community
Customers,
Employees
and Owners.

Bywater Technology has a neat way of showing the issues and relationships in *CCEO* priorities:

CUSTOMERS
Reliability
Predictability
Value for Money
On-time delivery
Problems Solved

COMMUNITY
No Environmental Risk
Job Opportunities
Facilities
Disposable Income
Predictability

TQM Organisation

Reward
Recognition
Safety and Security
Prospects
Positive Image

Return on Investment
Increased Asset Value
Predictability
Confidence
Positive Image

EMPLOYEES

OWNERS

Which of these is the most important? Put the Customers first, the Employees second and the Owners in last place. You might care to add a second '*C*' category, Community that can be used to capture issues involving your local community and the environment in which you operate.

At first sight it seems the wrong way round to put the owners in last place, but it is not. Satisfying customer expectations comes first, because without the customers, you go out of business. To allow these expectations to be met, you have then to provide the employees with the necessary tools, release their commitment and encourage motivation to allow customer expectations to be met. When you have done all that, profits rise and the owners are delighted.

Most owners of companies, particularly large ones, are simply shareholders, and they really don't care much about the people who work there. They care about profits and equity value, so they sit in last place, because, although their satisfaction is not necessarily easy to achieve, it is at least straightforward and provided by the results obtained from practising effective Total Quality Management.

Why are you in business? Ask most of your people, even the very senior ones, and many will say 'To make a profit'. Rubbish, I say, this is a confusion of cause and effect. You are in business to serve your customers with what they expect. No more, no less. If you do this efficiently, then the customer receives what he/she expects at a profit to your organisation.

Slice 65 Customer and Quality Awareness Surveys

65.1 Customer Surveys

The only point of these surveys is to find out what customers think of you, your products and your services, so they need to be well structured and the questions asked should be devised in such a way that the answers can be measured and analysed. It's no use asking 'Do you like us?', Because you will inevitably get some rude answers the only response to which can be 'sorry' or 'have a food parcel'.

Employ someone skilled, I hate to say it, but the word is consultant, who has experience in devising customer surveys. Make the survey anonymous, compare yourselves with your competitors, *believe* the results and ACT upon them quickly enough for your customers to connect their answers with your improvements.

Don't keep the data too secret, although personal remarks like 'Joe Bloggs could do with a bath before he comes to see me next time' should be kept between you and Joe.

Doing surveys, or polls as the politicians like to call them, is a sophisticated business and needs experienced people to conduct them. Otherwise, the answers can be meaningless. If you admit the survey is on your behalf, you run the risk of biased answers, in some cases in your favour or otherwise.

If you are a product manufacturer, a sensible set of issues to examine could be as follows:

- Product performance
- Product delivery, consistency and status advice
- Product safety and handling
- Response to complaints
- Technical problem solving and tools of quality
- Order handling efficiency
- Quality/knowledge of technical staff
- Quality/knowledge of logistics and commercial staff
- Value for money

- Product improvement ability
- Responsiveness and sensitivity of the whole company.

If you are a service company, then the questions will no doubt be different but the principles are the same, 'do your customers care about you?'

65.2 Quality Awareness Surveys

The trouble with quality is that most people are not aware of how to improve it. A 1991 European Foundation for Quality Management (EFQM)[18] survey of the top 500 Chief Executive Officers in Europe showed that quality is seen by 91% of them as an important issue, but only 15% saw it as a top corporate priority. CEO's are looking for reasons to say 'yes' but wanting to say 'no' but can't because it is not fashionable. They are not sure what's in it for them. Many of them could transform their competitive position and profitability by adopting TQM, but they don't know it.

A management survey done by Develin and Partners about factors that inhibit quality improvement, showed that while awareness of total quality is high, improvement (profitability) is depressingly low. The survey highlighted a number of factors which cause concern among the detractors of quality improvement processes:

- Problem of making enough time available.
- Difficulty of enhancing internal services.
- Lack of focus on the measurable benefits.
- Long-winded communication process.
- Weak inter-departmental knowledge.
- Cultural change problems.

Depressing isn't it? But as a friend of mine says 'Sorry about the facts, sorry about the facts'.

Slice 66 Market Changes

Changes in the market place can leave your business floundering. TQM can alert you to these changes because TQM is a process focused on the customers' expectations, so you should always know what he wants and needs. Do you remember the Swiss watch industry failing to adjust to electronic technology?

A survey showed that it costs five times as much to go out and get a new customer as to retain those you already have. Companies continue to spend millions of pounds seeking *new* customers through advertising and promotion while remaining oblivious to the fact that *current* customers are haemorrhaging out through the back door. The customer decides who wins and who loses. The old customers leave mainly because of service quality problems; it's rather like a leaky bucket.

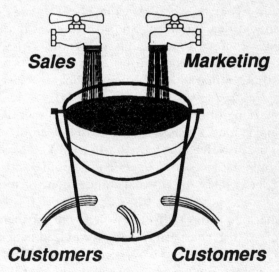

Sales   **Marketing**

Customers   **Customers**

If you plug the quality leaks, you can fill the bucket with customer satisfaction by working 'smarter rather than harder', thus using TQM as a competitive weapon.

Slice 67 Benchmarking

Best Practice Benchmarking (BPB) is a technique used by many successful companies to help them become as good as or better than the best in the world in their field of activity. BPB involves:

- Asking the customer to explain the difference between ordinary and excellent suppliers.
- Setting standards based on the best practices found.
- Finding out how the best organisations do it.
- Using your own and other organisations' ideas and methods to meet the standards set.

Benchmarking prevents the need to 're-invent the wheel'. Why invent it yourself when someone else is already doing it? The benefits of Benchmarking show themselves in: improved understanding of customers and competitors, fewer complaints, reduction in waste, earlier awareness of new innovations, a stronger market-place reputation, and last but not least, *more profit and sales*.

Benchmarking is a hard road to walk because it demands a positive open mind always willing to self-examine activities without constantly defending the status quo. You have to learn to share your methods and experiences, both good and bad with outsiders, where the normal stance is one of secrecy and defence.

Benchmarking is most effective when your partners are not competitors. When competitors talk, it can lead to accusations of cartel formation and, anyway, competitors talking together leads to a competition on who can tell the biggest lies!!

Slice 68 Important People

68.1 *Quality Consultants*

If you buy a Total Quality Management model from one of the many vendors, it will help you no end. It is the best way to start a TQM process because you get the whole structure, and hopefully the methodology, in one go. However, as you journey through this never ending process, you will realise that you have spent a lot of money on a system of common sense and may be tempted to feel it was not good value for money.

The more effective you make your TQM process, the more common sense it makes, and the greater the feeling that you should have done it yourself. But you didn't, did you? So it must have been worth it.

> **Who can, does.**
> **Who can't, teaches!**

Remember though,

> **A quality consultant is someone who borrows your watch to tell you what time it is!**

An additional depressing thought:

> *So much has been earned by so many and benefited so few!*

Quality Professionals are people usually educated beyond the point of common sense, blundering around in the quality maze (Slice 45) and complicating everything to a point where even they don't understand it any more.

They served a useful purpose once by inventing and promoting the concepts of TQ through the wilderness years when we all thought that quality was exclusively a production issue.

I knew they were insufferable dinosaurs when I first read the definition of quality (Slice 3), a clear example of a committee gone mad. So,

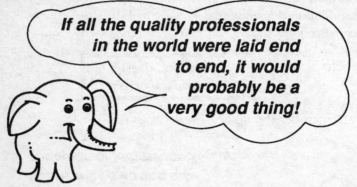

If all the quality professionals in the world were laid end to end, it would probably be a very good thing!

When the Quality Professionals finally come out of the back room and de-jargonise their subject, we will all benefit. Too much quality management starts with Statistical Process Control (SPC), continues with SPC and finishes with SPC.

Quality Professionals, bless them all, have much to their credit and otherwise.

TQM is about people, procedures, systems and action, not necessarily in that order, and should be treated as common sense, because it is.

Slice 69 The Case for Quality Costing

Quality Costs matter because:

- They are usually large (5% to 25% of sales revenue), but they are not usually measured by traditional methods. The result is that they are not known and, therefore, un-controlled.
- They allow you to pin-point areas of waste and thus set priorities for what to tackle first.

The purpose, therefore, of quality costing in your process of continuous quality improvement, is not only to set priorities, but if you are the budget holder, to give you an incentive and personal justification for making your quality process work. It will save you money, make you more competitive and provide greater job security for you and your people.

Monitoring quality through quality costing ensures that improvements are obtained without increasing costs. Belay the thought that quality improvement costs money. In reality quality is free, and your quality costing results will quickly show this to be so. It is obviously cheaper to do it right first time than to have to do it twice.

There are two well accepted and documented ways of recording your quality costs which are described in BS 6143: Guide to the economics of quality.

Part 1 is about the Process Analysis model.

Part 2 is about the PAF model, which means Prevention, Appraisal and Failure.

The PAF model does not take the efficiency of producing a product or service into consideration. Therefore, PAF contains a cost not involved in quality costing, which could be described as *the cost of running the business*.

69.1 Quality Costs – Process Analysis Model

The basis of Process Analysis is to understand the scope of the processes which make up a business' activity and to understand the relationship and interactions between the various activities of the process. This is usually done in the form of a flowchart.

When this is achieved, the cost of operating these processes can be analysed and calculated to obtain the Cost of Quality. Quality Cost measurement measures the gap between the *actual* costs of a business and its *potential* performance if every activity in the business is being carried out in accordance with requirements, first time and every time.

$$
\begin{aligned}
&\text{Let,} && \text{Total Quality Costs} = TQC \\
&\text{Let,} && \text{Cost of Conformance} = COC \\
&\text{Let,} && \text{Cost of non-Conformance} = CONC \\
&\text{Therefore,} && TQC = COC + CONC
\end{aligned}
$$

This is the Process Analysis model described in Part 1 of BS 6143: Guide to the economics of quality, published in 1992.

This method of quality costings means that the total cost of running the business is either part of COC or part of CONC. All costs are included somewhere.

Slice 70 Quality Costs – PAF Model

According to the PAF model, quality costs are divided into **Prevention Costs, Appraisal Costs, Internal Failure Costs** and **External Failure Costs**. If quality costing is not done right it can become a wild guess carried out to two decimal places. Get the accountants on your side to give quality costs official standing. Without the active, valuable and expert cooperation of the bean counters, your quality costs will be less accurate, less believable and will lack credibility and quickly fall into disrepute. The accountants are the only group of people who can make financial data official. Remember:

> *On the battlefield of business,*
> *the accountant is the guy*
> *going around*
> *shooting the wounded.*

Quality cost measurements are necessary to show your gross improvement in financial terms. Of great importance are those items which indicate improvements in customer satisfaction, the cost of non-conformance (CONC) and the items which break down into the cost categories shown above.

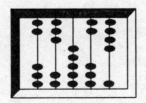

It is good to have the finance department on your side, and anyway, if you give them ownership of the quality costing system, they will do most of the work!

70.1 Quality Formulae – PAF Model

Some people like a mathematical approach to their day, so here goes:

Let,   Total Quality Costs $= TQC$

Let,   Prevention Investments $= PI$

Let,   Total Prevention Costs $= TPC$

Let,   Cost of Non-Conformance $= CONC$

Let,   Appraisal Costs $= AC$

Let,   Internal Failure Costs $= IFC$

Let,   External Failure Costs $= EFC$

Let 'x' be the fraction of Appraisal Cost which are Failure Costs

Therefore, $CONC = IFC + EFC + x(AC)$

and, $TPC = PI + (1-x)\,AC$

Therefore, $TQC = PI + (1-x)AC + IFC + EFC + x(AC)$
$$= CONC + TPC$$

If this helps you understand Quality Costing any better, then fine, otherwise, forget it.

This is the Prevention, Appraisal and Failure (PAF) model described in Part 2 of BS 6143: Guide to the economics of quality.

Slice 71 Quality Cost Numbers

Bywater Technology[15], says that every year industry loses money through poor service, delivery delays, wasted materials and lost opportunities. It is estimated that between 5% and 45% of turnover is lost in this way.

This waste, the difference in cost between what is done and what was planned, is the inevitable product of lax routines, ill-defined responsibilities, poor communications and a culture that accepts customer complaints, daily hassle, defective products and equipment failures as a regrettable but accept-able pattern of business life.

In the UK alone, some £15 billion is lost every year because of this culture. Individual managements should question themselves on their own share of this total.

The consequential costs of operating in an inefficient environment, the cost of the surprises caused by operating with informal routines and people not knowing what is expected of them, form the bulk of avoidable Quality Costs. On average, these costs run at 25% of sales; a major waste of people, materials, resources and profits. These surprises or unplanned events result in daily frustration, demotivated people and dissatisfied customers.

So what is the solution to these fire-fighting activities which cost our businesses so much? Total Quality Management is the solution.

71.1 Optimum Quality Costs

In the first flush of enthusiasm after some measurements of quality costs have been done, you may see all sorts of possible improvements. More inspection (Slice 46) may at first sight seem appropriate, but the trick of good quality cost management is to eliminate the possibility of errors by practising prevention techniques.

The following graph shows what can happen to quality costs and the disadvantages of practising too much inspection and not enough prevention. Failures go down, but costs can go up if the correct balance is not struck between the competing methodologies.

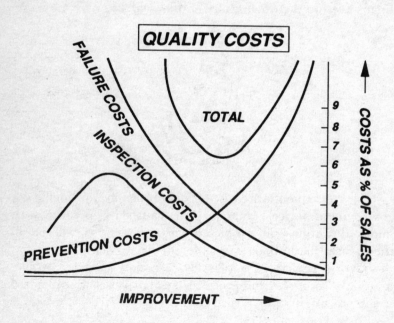

Slice 72 Reported Quality Costs

Most organisations tend to punish mistakes, sometimes brutally but mostly by more subtle means which can often be just as destructive. The consequence is that people sweep mistakes under the carpet, and the more senior the person with the broom, the higher the carpet gets. In consequence, your reported failure costs will inevitably be less than they really are.

As fear is driven out of the process of managing the business, and people can see problems as goldmines for improvement, they will report more of their failures and the reported cost of non-conformance will rise. Don't be depressed, this is normal. The real and reported costs of non-conformance will gradually converge and the total will begin to decline as your quality improvement process takes hold.

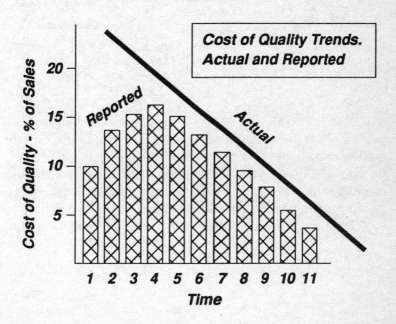

151

72.1 The Iceberg

Quality Costs can exceed 25% of sales revenue. You don't believe me? Then look at the diagram.

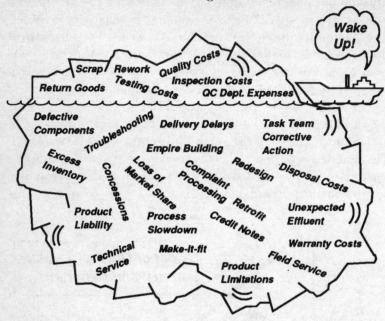

It's an iceberg, with 90% of the non-conformance costs hidden below the water line. Don't attempt to eliminate all the quality related costs, some of them, such as training, are very beneficial. Costs (investment might be a better word), like training should be encouraged, since they help prevent errors. When you are perfect, your Total Costs of Quality might drop to as little as 7% of sales value. Until then, keep working at it.

Slice 73 Measurement of Quality

Money is the usual system of measurement. It helps to manage the business, but traditional balance sheets rarely tell you much about quality. When you buy a washing machine, and it doesn't work, you want it fixed. Whether or not the supplier makes a profit in the end is not your concern. Conversely, saying 'we increased profits last month by 10%', gives little indication about customer satisfaction.

Certain costs (Slice 70) are related to quality, and these measurements show you how your quality improvement process is performing and help you identify critical issues which need addressing.

ICI Paints use the following criteria as Measurements of Customer Satisfaction:

- Delivery accuracy
- Invoice errors
- Right first time
- Lead times
- Telephone responses
- Suppliers deliveries
- Customer complaints/queries
- Bills of material accuracy
- Inventory record accuracy
- Forecasting accuracy
- Adjustments per batch

If you are in production management, you will certainly understand and use the concept of 'yield'. The concept of yield can be applied to customer satisfaction as well as production. It simply requires the need to define what 100% yield is, and aim for that.

73.1 Small Measurements

Of greater significance to the quality improvement process than issues such as Cost of Quality (Slice 70), are the thousands of small measurements which are often not expressed in financial terms. For example, the number of times the photocopier jams, analysis of complaints, number of credit notes, missed deadlines, customer surveys, paperwork errors, minutes late of meeting start, missed deliveries, overtime worked, training deficiencies, computer down-time, volume of effluent, adverse (and good) press reports, and so on.

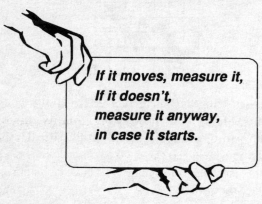

**If it moves, measure it,
If it doesn't,
measure it anyway,
in case it starts.**

Get your people to do their own measurements. Stick charts on the walls for all to see. It helps to make your quality improvement process more visible. People tend to set themselves goals when they see measured trends in the form of simple to understand graphs and charts. Everyone concerned wants to see the line of the graph go in the right direction.

To see	To perceive	To interpret
I see it	What is it?	What does it mean?

More and more slices, yes?

Slice 74 Quality Standards

I promised not to mention ISO 9000/BS 5750, well at least not too often. This particular set of standards has been devised to encourage organisations to write down what they do and how they do it. ISO 9000 is an excellent tool within your quality process, because it helps you identify the 'goldmines' for improvement (Slice 25). The standard does not demand that you improve, it simply demands that you document your procedures for getting things done.

If you make rubbish, then say so, but maybe in not so many words.

Remember though, if you aren't careful you can institutionalise your inefficiencies by casting them in concrete and quite happily and consistently achieve these inefficiencies year after year.

ISO 9000 is about *procedures* and TQM is about *people*. If you improve the former and motivate the latter you will have an organisation better able to survive in this increasingly discriminating world. ISO 9000 is a tool for use in TQM processes and should not be seen as an end in itself.

One nice thing about deciding to go for ISO 9000 certification, is that there is a clear goal at the end of it with a certificate from an external body saying that you have done and complied with certain requirements and activities. It affects everybody.

If you are now nodding in agreement, then fine. But, remember, you should run the whole of your TQM process on these lines. Short- and long-term goals and recognition for teams, departments, locations, divisions, businesses, countries and continents are an essential part of effective TQM, not just for ISO 9000 certification.

There is another important quality standard dealing with Cost of Quality (Slice 70).

74.1 Performance Standards

Defect-free goods and services can only be expected when

155

performance standards exist which all the people involved can understand. Setting these performance standards needs to involve all the people and should be an integral part of your planning process.

I bought a new house some years ago and the shower tray was made of plastic. After a few months it began to leak and the whole fiasco cost more than £500 to fix. The reason was simple, the person who fitted the shower tray had not adjusted the supporting feet under the tray. The cost would have been an extra two minutes.

But that was not the fundamental reason for the problem. The builder who hired him as a contractor to fit shower trays in several hundred similar houses, had not set a suitable performance standard.

People need the skills to do what they are supposed to do, preceded and followed by a management which cares about the results. To achieve this, you need performance standards aimed at error free products and services and a philosophy of 'Right Every Time'.

74.2 *Will you?*

Have you got the guts to take one department where errors keep occurring and fix by preventive measures every error one by one so that they don't happen again? Minute by minute, hour by hour, day by day until it all works properly?

It might take ages to do this, and when it all works as it's supposed to do, will you move onto the next department and do it all over again?

And will you be there throughout, encouraging, helping, mentoring, cajoling, insisting and teaching to show you care that it works?

Will you -
'Care because you dare?'

Will you never allow excuses, never assign blame, never be inconsistent and never say die? Will you lead from the front? If you want TQM to work, you will have to do this, there is no better way because you have to:

> **Lead YOUR quality process**

Slice 75 Assessing Quality Improvement

Your progress in quality improvement needs to be measured in a variety of ways if you are to avoid blind-alleys and make good priorities. Quality Costs (Slice 70), and many other measurements are needed. Not least of these is a method of self-assessment of the progress of the overall improvement process.

Several hundred thousand copies of the Malcolm Baldridge National Quality Award booklet have been distributed in the United States. No doubt the same will happen with the European Foundation for Quality Management in Europe. Most of the companies requesting the booklets have no intention of applying for the award. They use the information for self-assessment.

One of the pitfalls of self assessment is the tendency to cut corners and indulge in 'wish-listing'. When you have reached a stage in your quality improvement process where you have made very real progress and it shows, this might be the moment to consider applying for one of the external awards.

There are specific procedures for doing this, which include notification of the intention to apply, internal assessment, submission of a report and a site visit by the examining team.

75.1 European Foundation for Quality Management

A method of measuring your performance in a consistent and systematic way, utilises the criteria and guidelines of the European Foundation for Quality Management (EFQM) described in the booklet entitled 'The European Quality Award'[18].

Each of the criteria carries a maximum number of points which total 1000 when all the categories are added together.

The criteria are divided into 'enablers' and 'results' and are similar to the Malcolm Baldridge National Quality Award used in the USA.

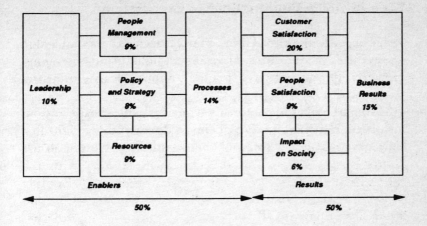

	People Management 9%			Customer Satisfaction 20%	
Leadership 10%	Policy and Strategy 8%	Processes 14%		People Satisfaction 9%	Business Results 15%
	Resources 9%			Impact on Society 6%	

Enablers · Results

← 50% → ← 50% →

75.2 *The Malcolm Baldridge National Quality Award*

A similar method of assessment has existed in the United States since 1987. The seven categories of assessment include:

- Leadership (100)
- Information and analysis (70)
- Strategic quality planning (60)
- Human resource utilisation (150)
- Quality assurance of products and services (140)
- Quality results (180)
- Customer satisfaction (300)

The maximum points score per category is shown in brackets. The seven categories break down into 32 items each of which has different areas that have to be addressed.

The scoring is based upon evaluating each item from the point of view of how the organisation has approached the subject, how it has deployed its resources and the results obtained.

Slice 76 100% Conformance to Expectations

In his book, Right First Time[1], Frank Price talks at great length about the 'OK' questions related to manufacturing operations. However, these questions are equally applicable to administrative procedures.

If you are going to conform to your customers' expectations all the time then you have to aim to do everything right first time every time. So some of the questions you need to ask yourself are:

- CAN we do it OK?
- ARE we doing it OK?
- HAVE we done it OK?
- COULD we do it better?

Nothing less than 100% conformance to expectations of customers both internal and external can be the goal. Don't confuse expectations with specifications either. Specifications are about 'needs'. Expectations are about 'wants + needs'. A man called Alan Cowan once defined a specification as, '*a*

A specification is a document written with a pen dipped in tears.

document written with a pen dipped in tears'. It can go horribly wrong if the specification does not embrace the real needs and wants of the customer whether she be your largest contributor to revenue or a clerk down the corridor.

76.1 When 99.9% Right isn't right enough

You cannot say 80%, 90% or 99% is OK because your people will say, 'I'm doing well, six mistakes a week around here is acceptable. I used to make ten, but now I only make six'.

You have to aspire to 100% right all the time. No other number will do. You cannot write down, *'we will aim for 90% or 99%'*, because they are limited targets. You would be saying, *'it's good enough'*. Nothing less than perfect can be your goal. Look at the consequences of only getting things 99.9% right.

- 1 hour/month of unsafe drinking water
- 2 unsafe landings/day at Heathrow Airport
- 10 babies/day dropped by doctors
- 100 incorrect surgical operations/week
- 1000 babies/year given to the wrong parents
- 3000 pieces of lost mail/hour
- 25000 mismatched pairs of shoes sold per year
- 30000 missed heartbeats/person/year.
- 40000 incorrect medical prescriptions/year

Slice 77 Right First Time

If you organise your activities in such a way that you can do everything right first time every time, job satisfaction rises dramatically. It is frustrating for people to spend time fixing mistakes. If the mistakes are their own it is hard enough, but if they are someone else's it is very demotivating and, of course, it takes more time.

> *Whoever wants to finish*
> *something*
> *quickly, must do it*
> *right first time round.*
>
> *John Young*

Two people were poring over a large computer printout, you know, the two feet wide music ruled lavatory paper we seem to get every so often. The information was rubbish. One person said thoughtfully to other, 'Without a computer, it would take three people almost four years to make a mistake this big'. Message:

If you're going

to make mistakes,

use a computer,

it's quicker.

There are people who spend their whole working lives simply correcting other peoples' mistakes.

> *To err is human,*
> *but to really foul things up,*
> *you need a computer.*

77.1 Benefits of Right First Time

Satisfied customers tell 3–5 of their friends, colleagues or other companies. Dissatisfied customers tell more than 10 friends, colleagues or other companies. It is a trait of human nature that we get more fun out of moaning than congratulating, particularly at work.

When was the last time you heard on the TV or radio news that Marks and Spencer got it right first time more often than not? If they kept getting it wrong it would be headlines all round. Good news spreads less far and fast than bad news, which should provide us all with a great incentive to improve ourselves and our businesses.

It should be our goal not only to do it right first time, but also to go one further and 'delight' the customer, as Deming said. By so doing the customer might tell more people how good we are. Surely this is the best type of advertising.

Slice 78 Small Steps and Often

Small steps and often is a better way to produce controlled evolutionary improvement than large, often unpredictable steps. The Japanese call it Kaizen, which can mean, 'transformation to the better' but the word has many other subtle overtones. In practise, Kaizen means that improvement is a continuous part of the job and demands a different type of management and supervisory thinking. Supervisors become team leaders and educators; managers become enablers providing resources and direction. An example of a simple small step improvement is as follows:

Step 1.   Put a piece of paper on one table and a pencil on a separate table.
Step 2.   Pick up the pencil and draw a circle on the paper.
Step 3.   Put the paper on a third table.

Question:

'Did you do it right this time?'

Answer: probably 'yes' unless you are dim.

Now, make one improvement.

Step 1.   Put both the pencil and paper on the same table.
Step 2.   Repeat the exercise and put the paper on the same table.

Question: 'Did you do it right this time?'
Answer: 'yes'.

Step 1. Put the pencil and paper on separate tables again.
Step 2. Repeat the first exercise.

Question: 'Did you do it right this time.'
Answer: 'Yes, but not as good as last time'.

So the real issue is, 'Did you do it right this time?', or, 'Did you do it better this time?', and finally, 'Can you do it right every time?' Accomplish your continuous quality improvements in small steps and often.

78.1 The Bear Facts

But let's be realistic, you can't expect perfection immediately or even in the fairly long term. Initially, we are in a race and being noticeably better than the competition can be a worthwhile goal. Leave perfection for later.

A Japanese gentleman and an American were wandering along in Grisly bear country when in the distance they saw a Grisly hurtling towards them. The American turned to run, but the man from Nippon sat on the ground and took out his running shoes from his haversack.

'Come on,' pleaded the American, 'You can't run faster than a Grisly'.

'I don't have to,' replied the Japanese, 'I only have to run faster than you'.

Slice 79 Mistake-Proofing

Shigeo Shingo (Slice 10) taught Statistical Process Control for 20 years before he realised that it was the wrong starting pointing.

Why?

Because Statistical Process Control accepts that things can be wrong and can go wrong. Shingo started to put mistake-proofing in first place which he calls Poka-Yoke or 'Defect=0', but mistake-proofing devices will do for us.

If you work hard and effectively, but in isolation, to prevent mistakes, you are not likely to feel appreciated. However, if the Chief Executive Officer repeatedly says,

'There is no activity more important than preventing mistakes, because I am personally dedicated to the goal of 100% conformance to our customers' expectations and mistake-proofing is an integral part of the achievement of this goal',

then everybody wants to join and people do not feel isolated. They feel part of the team when they make personal improvements.

We need to organise and then behave in a way which allows the mistake-proofing concepts of Shigeo Shingo to actually happen. They are an attitude of mind or a slogan. Shingo applied the concept mainly to production processes, but it is equally applicable to administrative or sales procedures. Source Inspection can be implemented using Poka-Yoke devices which are, therefore, a tool of Source Inspection.

Source Inspection checks for factors which cause errors, not for the defects which can result. For example, if you keep putting a part on a machine the wrong way round, redesign the part so that it can only be put on the right way round. A variety of tools are available to help detect these 'Sources of error' which result in Zero-Defects by making it impossible to do the task wrongly.

166

79.1 Fool-proof Design

The top of the box below has symmetrical holes and can be fitted the wrong way round. Redesign it with asymmetrical holes, so that it cannot be fitted the wrong way round.

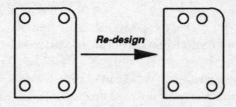

It seems simple because it is, but it is still the wrong way. Don't re-design it, but design it correctly in the first place. This takes planning, time, effort, imagination and the will to have it right before you produce it. It's no good being diligent during your production process when the design is wrong, because it is already too late.

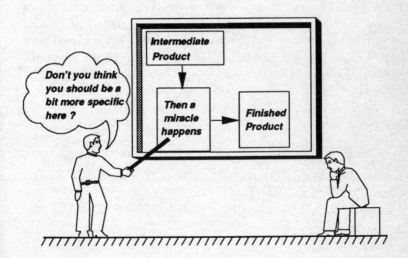

Slice 80 Details are a Bitch but Necessary

There is not very much involved in running a TQM process. You teach your people the philosophy and tools, organise them into teams, and reap the benefits.

That's all there is to it really, apart from a few million details.

Each time you tackle a repeat of a task done before, or plan a new task, prepare a check-list of all the actions and thoughts necessary to do it right first time. You will be surprised how many items you need for apparently simple activities.

Far too many top managers believe they need only concern themselves with strategy and organisation; details are for lower forms of life to deal with. This lack of attention to the details by top managers leads to the erection of barriers for operational people to jump over, hoops to dive through and demeaning rules which demotivate their people. In other words, top managers are uninvolved because they never get their coats off and find out how the system really works.

For example, running a teaching workshop requires about 600 individual items that need to be thought about and acted upon. They are not trivial, because each is important in its own way. The lack of a spare light bulb for the overhead projector can really spoil your day when the one in use blows.

80.1 *TQM Books*

Only read one, then do it. They all say the same things since TQM is common sense, tarted up by etymological experts into tomes of wisdom unashamedly plagiarised from everybody else. This book is no exception, except that it is thinner!!

To reach this conclusion, I did read a few books myself, which you will find listed in the Bibliography.

Slice 81 Effective Communication

A picture is worth a thousand words.

Goal: To make a Swing

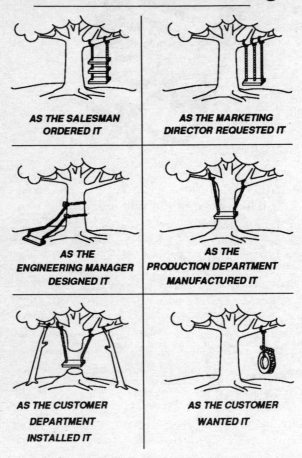

AS THE SALESMAN
ORDERED IT

AS THE MARKETING
DIRECTOR REQUESTED IT

AS THE
ENGINEERING MANAGER
DESIGNED IT

AS THE
PRODUCTION DEPARTMENT
MANUFACTURED IT

AS THE CUSTOMER
DEPARTMENT
INSTALLED IT

AS THE CUSTOMER
WANTED IT

There is nothing more important to your action process than getting your communications right. Good communication is a great motivator, avoids misunderstandings and reduces your Cost of Quality by avoiding mistakes.

Good TQM needs to be relentlessly communicated, but what needs communicating? Successes, for example. Good communication is a two-way process. Simply writing memoranda is information, not communication and the scope for misunderstanding is limitless. If your message lacks clarity and truth you may go down all sorts of blind alleys and make horrendous mistakes.

Archduke Ferdinand found alive, first world war a mistake.

If you want your people to believe your message and do something with it, go talk to them. If I have something to say to my wife, I don't write her a memo, I sit down with her and talk about it. Yet many managers have a communications culture based on *management by memorandum*. Some things are best done in writing, like the monthly pay-slip, but others are best done face to face.

Ask yourself this, 'How often have I had something important to communicate and used my Personal Computing Blunderbuss (PCB) instead of my mouth?' It's so easy to use the PCB, but is it the most appropriate way in this case?

What is a Personal Computing Blunderbuss? This is a computer able to mail shot people with standard information tarted up so it looks like it's just for them. It works once or twice but eventually people know how impersonal it really is.

171

Slice 82 Relentless Communication

If you are to keep your quality process alive, particularly in the early stages, make it visible. If people don't know what is going on and they cannot see it, they are inclined to think it is dead. Be prepared to treat the early stages of your TQM process like an advertising campaign for a new product or service. Remember, doing without advertising is like winking at a pretty girl in a dark room. You know what you're doing but nobody else does.

Make people aware of what is going on by making your TQM process visible using posters, quality bulletin boards, newsletters (not just on quality), quality buttons and pins.

For some reason, door mats with quality messages are particularly effective at getting a message over. Use your recognition system for teams and individuals as a method of communicating your quality messages. Make a fuss about it and organise events that reinforce your process; quality days, for example.

Don't let your TQM process operate in the background, no matter how effective it may seem; relentlessly communicate it to all your people. And don't just advertise successes, go and explain, listen and modify.

82.1 The Grapevine

Employee surveys repeatedly show that the most believed and avidly attended information source is the grapevine. Therefore, management should get plugged in. The people may as well believe the facts, rather than make it up for themselves.

Remember to tell the truth though. If you don't they will find you out. TQM is not about always giving people a rosy story; if there is bad news to impart, tell them. Your good news is then more believable.

> In God we trust, everybody else
> must bring data.
> J S Bigelow, Exxon Chemicals
> America

It is not possible to use the grapevine as a simple extension to your regular communication methods. It needs a concerted and orchestrated effort to go and talk to people face to face (Slice 20). The grapevine will operate no matter what you do, so it may as well be based on facts.

Slicing nicely, yes?

Slice 83 Training

Management personnel often have a tendency to regard training as something to do later; it can always be delayed. Many managers think that their people can't learn.

Take for example those bulky machines that retailers and restaurants use for imprinting credit card details onto the multi-part payment dockets. The machines weigh a ton (do you believe that)? No, they weigh less than a kilo but they are still muscle developers, but used only to position the card on the docket and imprint the embossed characters onto the paper. British Rail has greater faith in their dining car money collectors. They use the barrel of their ball-point pen to rub across the docket. It works just as well and relieves them of the need to use the muscle developers.

Mind you, BR isn't perfect at training. I saw two well-dressed waitresses pushing and pulling a trolley up the aisle of the first class dining car full of well-heeled business people eating their expensive breakfast. The pusher said to the puller in a loud voice, '. . . and it gets me into trouble every bloody time.' A totally out of place remark, and everybody in earshot noticed. The lady needed training in the art of customer sensitivity.

As Peter Sellers once said,

> *'Some of these people have never had a lesson in their lives'.*

International Computers Limited say they spend at least 9 days per year per employee on training, and regard this as a minimum. How much training time do your people get?

British Rail has certainly got the message in some quarters about informing the passengers about the journey. I can hear the trainer saying, 'Tell them which train they are on. Be friendly. Tell them what you're doing'. Unfortunately he didn't go far enough with one guard on my Intercity train.

'Good mornin' ladies and gennelmen', I am Trevor Clegg and this is the Intercity Service from Manchester Piccadilly to London Euston, calling at Stockport, Macclesfield and Rugby. Welcome to the passengers *what* have just joined us at Stockport'.

Message: Don't leave things to chance. Be thorough, train people properly in a workshop atmosphere and pay lots of attention to detail. Otherwise, you could do more harm than good.

Beware of the character who says, 'What?, I'm too bright to need to learn anything.'

Slice 84 Training Subjects

Specific jobs require specialised training like book-keeping, pump-maintenance and gay-rights activist. There are courses to teach these subjects at colleges and universities. They are generally not undertaken as in-house training. However, if your switchboard operator answers the telephone without a smile on her face, it will show in her manner. She deserves to be trained in 'charm' and the more specific needs of the job, such as what to say when an outside call comes in. 'Hullo' will not do, she needs to say who the organisation is. Remember, switchboard operators are your front line to the market place, but who bothers to train them?

Some of the training specific to good TQM includes;

- Quality awareness
- Team building
- Team leader and member training
- Supplier assessment
- Chairmanship
- Effective delegation
- Time management.

- Problem sharing and solving
- Consulting-, listening-, and mentoring-skills
- Presentation skills
- The tools of quality
- Leadership
- Dealing with difficult people

Only you can make a complete list, which depends on the skills and characteristics of your organisation.

84.1 Training Manuals

These are best written by a simpleton. Bright people like computer programmers and people with a PhD who have been educated beyond the point of common sense, can't write instructions in ways which ordinary humans can follow precisely.

176

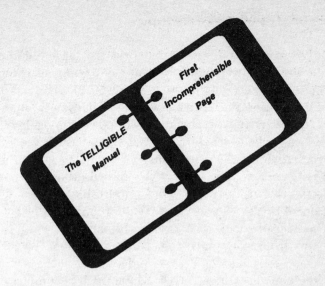

After the practical simpleton has written the manual, don't forget to test it on someone.

I was teaching someone how to use a simple computer programme and asked the trainee to follow the screen instructions. She fluttered her fingers above the keyboard for a few seconds and did nothing. I said, 'go on then, do it'. She said, 'I can't do it, I can't find the ANY key'. I rest my other case.

Slice 85 Training Workshops

Adult education and training are best accomplished in participative groups. In general, you are not going to teach them academic subjects, but practical subjects. Therefore, participation, illustration and a fun atmosphere drives the point home in the most effective way. This is a workshop atmosphere.

For example, to teach the principles of TQM, the following characteristics typify a workshop.

- 15–25 participants
- Letter of introduction
- Lots of breaks
- Changes of pace
- Away from work place
- Group exercises
- Pre-defined seating
- Case histories
- Own people as trainers
- Brief slides with big text
- Pre-defined group discussions.

- U-shaped table
- Comfortable chairs
- Well organised
- No hitches
- No interruptions
- Videos
- Move them around
- Ask questions
- Good presentation skills
- Posters with messages

And Humour:

Be thankful for problems, if they were less difficult, someone else with less ability might have your job!

Slice 86 Job Descriptions

In principle, I hate them, but they are a necessary evil, particularly for large companies. Job descriptions can be helpful in identifying training needs, but do make them practical and specific so that the gap between needed skills and present skills can be clearly seen at annual appraisal time. Job descriptions are a useful means of defining who is responsible for RESULTS.

Your quality process will insist that people are trained and refreshed often. Good job descriptions can not only help with training needs but also with the changes necessary to the nature of the job being described. Lawler divided job characteristics into five components.

Skill variety. What are the demands that the job makes on the person doing it?

Task Identity. Does what he is doing make sense to him?

Significance. Does it matter if he does it properly or not as described? Is the job really necessary in its current form?

Autonomy. Can he exercise judgement and discrimination over the way he does the job?

Feedback. Does he get to know if he is doing it right or not?

When you evaluate jobs using these criteria and find that they get a very low score, don't assume that the job is worthless. There is every probability that you didn't describe the job properly in the first place. I have heard of cases such as car park attendants getting a terribly low score. It's not surprising that they may not be turned on much about what they are required to do because they don't feel valued.

If your car were damaged in a car park, you would soon raise your opinion of the value of the job, if the car park attendant pasted on your windscreen the car number of the animal who did it!

Lawlor's five criteria is a good way to ensure well constructed and 'active' job descriptions.

179

Slice 87 Quality Losses

85% of quality losses are management correctable and only 15% of these losses are worker related. The 85% are usually system failures and stay in the system until reduced or eliminated by management. The 15% are special causes and sometimes specific to certain employees.

These losses are not easily translatable into money. How do you measure loss of market share due to the often poor attitude of some sales people and other employees who come into contact with your external customers? You cannot easily measure how much business you lost or failed to gain due to these factors. But they are still losses due to quality errors. Don't forget that surveys show the reasons why customers stop buying from you:

    5% die, retire, get fired, or move to other jobs

    5% give the business to their friends

    10% stop buying for competitive reasons

    15% because of product dissatisfaction and

    65% because of a *bad-attitude from suppliers' employees*.

In addition, dissatisfied customers are rather more likely to spread bad news than good, so problems of bad service compound themselves.

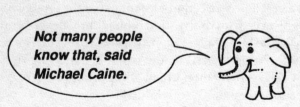

Not many people know that, said Michael Caine.

The internal losses associated largely with management methods and attitudes can be quantified and corrected and make up an important part of internal failure costs (Slice 70).

Slice 88 The Action Checklist

When you have been running your process about a year and most of the people have received their initial training, ask yourself some questions then go FACE to FACE with a few other people and ask them these questions.

1. Has everybody attended a TQM workshop? How many of them?
2. Is everybody on a TQM team? How many?
3. What are your Vision statement, Quality Policy and Critical Success Factors for your department?
4. What are your critical quality issues?
5. What does your Annual Quality Plan require?
6. What are your Projects to support the Critical Success Factors?
7. How many of your people are participating in an Improvement Project?
8. How did you push decision making downward?
9. How do you verify the Critical Success Factors and measure the results of TQM activities?
10. How much are your Quality Costs?
11. What do your internal customers expect of you?
12. What do your external customers expect of you?
13. How does your Quality communication system work?
14. How much time do you spend on Management By Walking About?
15. Do you discuss Quality Improvements at meetings?
16. Do you use any of the Quality Tools? Which ones?
17. What are the fundamentals of TQM?
18. How do you encourage Right First Time?
19. How do you reward/recognise good performance?

Notice that the questions are framed in such a way that more than 'yes' or 'no' answers are required. Too threatening? Ask them anyway.

Slice 89 Reward and Recognition

89.1 Reward

Progress and change need to be reinforced by sharing the benefits of success with those who have helped to achieve it. Improved performance has led many organisations towards more flexible and individual reward schemes. Money is important but is not the sole or primary criterion influencing employee motivation. Job satisfaction, job security and opportunities to develop new skills are often equal to monetary rewards in an employee's scale of values.

However, money based rewards include:

- Merit pay
- Cash bonuses
- Profit related pay
- Employee share ownership
- Incentives/awards
- Recognition of Employee initiative.

Simply saying 'Thank you' can often be enough. It does not have to be monetary reward. People do not get out of bed each day only for the money. People do not want to do a bad job. Most of them are decently obligated to come to work and earn their pay. As Frank Price said, 'Since the company pays wages to the whole man, it makes sense to use as much of him as possible, as he leaves none of himself at home when he comes to work'.

Remember that people don't work for companies, profit centres or business units, they work for people in places and their reward comes from the appropriate actions of the people they work with. However, too much reward can also be a demotivating influence.

89.2 Recognition

Some form of recognition is desirable when people have done something special or different. Reward for day to day work comes in the form of a pay cheque. When people have been through a training course, give them, say, a certificate of achievement or a quality pin, but at least something.

I heard of a 60 year old cleaning lady who worked 30 years for a brewery chain and who went on a Customer Care course. After the course, the participants were given a certificate. To many people it was of little importance, but to the cleaning lady it was very important. When she was presented with her certificate, she brought her children and grand-children along. She was so proud; she had never before in her life received a formal qualification.

If you are going to recognise individuals with awards, don't forget to let all the people choose the winners in a secret ballot.

The winners will be much more impressed with selection by their peers than by selection through management. Don't rush into it; wait until something of significance happens, but, remember, TQM must be continually refuelled otherwise it will fall out of the sky.

Slice 90 Quality Awards

90.1 Quality Events

At intervals, as the TQM process progresses, organise quality events, such as quality days, or quality evenings where some of the benefits are shared with all the people in a fun and relaxed atmosphere.

Quality Events help management reaffirm their commitment to the quality process and should be dignified but also exciting and something for people to remember.

A good buffet lunch and a few drinks can go a long way to showing how much you appreciate the efforts of your people. But make sure you have something to crow about, and beware of the elephant copulation effect:

A lot of trumpeting and no results for two years.

90.2 Suggestion Schemes and Annual Quality Award Schemes

The conventional suggestion scheme found in many companies will be of little help in the future, because no organisation will be able to allocate enough people to revise and evaluate *all* the ideas generated. This could total as many as 10-15 per person per year (some companies in a far away sushi-land, not mentionable here, get many more). The solution is teams of people who become problem solvers and who need to be able to use the tools of quality.

Another conceptual problem with many suggestion schemes is that they emphasise ideas and rewards for individuals. TQM is more about teams than individuals. Further, schemes which reward financially for good ideas, encourage some people to feel that TQM will deprive them of their just rewards. TQM should foster an atmosphere of cooperation and improvement from everyone for the common good of the customers, employees and owners and not link these improvements to short-term cash.

90.3 Annual Quality Award Schemes

These are internal organisation schemes and not to be confused with the EFQM and the Malcolm Baldridge National Quality Awards, (Slice 75).

Annual Quality Awards, which go mainly to quality improvement teams, work much better than conventional suggestion schemes. A suggested outline could be as follows.

Award Categories
1. Most Benefit to External Customers
2. Most Benefit to Internal Customers
3. Most Innovative Improvement
4. Greatest Cost Saving

Guidelines
1. Awards will be made to a Quality Improvement Team in each category each year.
2. Each person on the site will have one vote for each category.
3. Each award will be to the value of £(keep it small) and will normally be divided equally among the team members.

Slice 91 Meetings

Don't make your TQM process bureaucratic. Don't make it into an endless series of Quality Steering Team meetings, quality circles, quality meeting this and quality meeting that ... Discuss ideas, issues for a few minutes to get one more action step, then go away and 'do it'.

Meetings are an institution in which the minutes are kept and the hours are thrown away.

Avoid calling the groups who are meeting, committees. It makes more people want to join. The more people who are involved, the more they all want to have a say and the more time can be wasted for the rest.

> A committee will always produce a compromise decision, the quality of which will be less good than each of the members could have produced on their own.

Incidentally, when you have a meeting about procedures in your factory or general office, do you invite factory operators or clerks to the meeting? If not, then I suppose you must be entirely familiar with their work procedures, right?

91.1 Meeting Review Sheet

The quality of meetings varies considerably. One way of improving them is to follow the measurement principle of TQM, 'What gets measured gets done'. Why not ask people at meetings to fill in the attached form after each meeting, ask the scribe to evaluate the answers (anonymously of course) and report the results at the next meeting. I guarantee that the quality of the meeting will improve.

Name of Meeting: **Name of Chairman:**
Date: **Duration:**

	Number of people present:	Max	Score
1	Did the meeting start and finish on time and was it free from interruptions? *Comments:	5	
2	Did arrangements meet requirements? (Meeting room, flip-charts, etc) *Comments:	5	
3	Was agenda and reading matter circulated on time? (ie one week in advance) *Comments:	10	
4	Was purpose of meeting clear? *Comments:	15	
5	Was a Chairman/Secretary appointed, was the timetable adhered to and was the meeting well controlled? *Comments:	10	
6	Did the meeting produce satisfactory actions/follow-up plan/minutes? *Comments:	10	
7	Were the right people there and did everyone make balanced contributions? *Comments:	10	
8	Were notes on previous meetings circulated on time and were actions completed? *Comments:	15	
9	Were people well prepared. Eg. Had they done the pre-reading and brought the relevant papers? *Comments:	10	
10	Did you benefit from the meeting and was it helpful for the business? *Comments:	10	
	TOTAL		
			%

Slice 92 Partnership Sourcing

If you wish to introduce programmes such as Just-in-time, then start partnerships with your suppliers. *Partnership sourcing* places quality above quantity, and helps to remove adversarial relationships. The system only works for large suppliers. The knee-jerk reaction to supplier mistakes is to find a new supplier. In partnership sourcing you find out what went wrong and then find a way to prevent it happening again. The benefits of Partnership Sourcing are to:

- Cut lead times
- Reduce stocks
- Better planning
- Reduce production down time and many others.

Traditional sourcing of goods and service relies largely on the sales person dealing with most customer contact about non-routine logistical issues. Each department within an organisation deals with the appropriate department of the supplier.

Traditional Sourcing

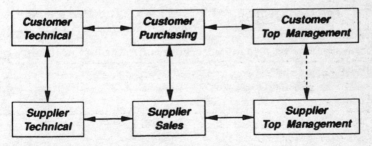

In the case of Partnership Sourcing, both customer and supplier form their own teams and the teams come together to discuss the customer-supplier relationship. They meet on a regular basis and avoid surprises through the department/ person called 'measurement'. This ensures that problems from both sides are properly discussed. The assembly and presence of the data are an integral part of the discussions, and makes it much more likely that problems are solved in a positive way. Partnership sourcing avoids the knee-jerk reaction of complaining and threatening when things go wrong. First, find out why it happened, then decide how to handle it.

Partnership Sourcing

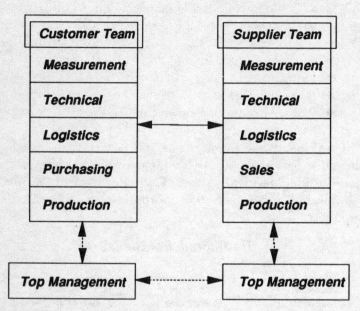

You operate as a team with your supplier for 'mutuality of benefit'.

Slice 93 Value for Money

Doing things better, doing things right first time, meeting customers' expectations and 'delighting' the customer are not inconsistent with lower costs. It does not necessarily cost more money to provide a better range of goods and services.

However, you cannot provide a Rolls Royce for the price of a Mini and there is a direct relationship between Quality, Quantity and Cost. In principle, a well-run organisation will have lower costs when it makes more of the same item because of economies of scale. It is essential that you educate your customers to understand what they can *reasonably* expect. They can fairly expect a discount for quantity but it is *unreasonable* to expect to buy higher and higher quality goods in smaller and smaller quantities at lower and lower prices without some long-term changes in efficiency. You know it and the customer knows it.

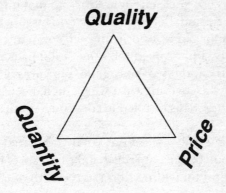

You and they must strike a balance between the three issues and this should be an integral part of your marketing programme. But remember, surveys show that the average customer will pay *more* for higher quality goods and services delivered on time.

93.1 Service First

In the 1960's I helped to develop a 'complete system' to prevent the caking of fertiliser granules. You wouldn't believe how irate a farmer gets when the fertiliser spreading machine blocks up and he has to get off his tractor. We only sold one component of the chemical anti-caking mix, albeit the critical one, but it seemed sensible to me to obtain details in the form of data sheets, catalogues, names and addresses of suppliers, of all the other components and the equipment to be used. This was done as a 'service' to the customer but helped us become expert on the process as a whole. My colleagues said I was crazy. Why help the other suppliers of components and equipment? This they said was the customer's job. I went through a period of discomfort about it, but my instincts said 'Do it'. The result was that the customers never made a move without asking me what I thought. We controlled the process and sales and profits grew.

Eventually, my boss insisted that we stop all this 'service'. Sales and margins fell and my boss said, it simply showed that our process was not good enough. 'Stick to making and selling the chemicals', he said, 'let the customer do his job, and we'll do ours. Service is for banks and insurance companies.'

More recently, I have used the same 'total package' concept in the oil industry and it worked again. The message is that you have to care for the customer in a way which meets not only his stated needs but also his implied needs; you have to *conform to his expectations*.

Of course, a cynic would say that I created unrealistic expectations; but I don't agree!! It takes all sorts of people to make a world and they often don't agree with one another.

Thank God for that, say I.

Bye.

It's not all sliced yet.

Acceptable Quality Level (AQL). The maximum percent defective (or maximum number of defects per hundred units) that, for purposes of acceptance sampling, can be considered satisfactory as a process average.

Acceptance Sampling Plan. A specific plan that states the sample size to be used and the associated acceptance and rejection criteria.

Action Team. See Corrective Action Team. See Quality Improvement Team. See Project Team.

Annual Quality Improvement Plan. A working document prepared by the operating committee of a company, organisation, division, staff group or subsidiary that addresses the critical quality issues on a project-by-project basis. It is a fundamental element of the Total Quality Management Process that moves the quality improvement process forward. It is part of the strategic business plan and is reviewed by top management on a regular basis. Each function, department or group develops action plans, resources, and progress review dates to accomplish the specific improvement projects.

Audit. An independent review conducted to compare some aspect of performance with a standard for that performance.

Brainstorming. Another name for Nominal Group Technique.

Business Unit Total Quality Function. A staff function that will track, measure and support the process that the Quality Steering Team has developed and the site teams are implementing. The function spearheads the movement away from inspection and compliance, to prevention and improvement.

CAT. See Corrective Action Team. See Quality Action Team. Also known as a small furry animal.

Cause and Effect Diagram. Also called the Fishbone Diagram or Ishikawa Diagram. An orderly, graphic form to show the arrangement of theories. A method of representing the relationship between some 'effect' and the possible 'causes' influencing it. From this activity, proposals are made to test the best theories through experimentation.

193

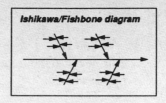

Ishikawa/Fishbone diagram

Champion. A highly recognised leader, who will visibly support the quality improvement process. A champion must be a leader who can make it happen, be a mentor and provide guidance, and act as a change agent.

Check Sheet. A tool used to gather data based on observations in order to begin to detect patterns.

Conformance. To bring performance into agreement with the customer's expectation, requirements, or specifications. Performance to prescribed standards.

Conformance to Customer Requirements (Specifications). A product driven quality philosophy which is difficult to differentiate from competition, since each manufacturer must meet requirements to have the minimum generic product.

Consistent Conformance to Customer Expectations. A total business and management quality philosophy, that focuses on product and service to the customer to satisfy not only her needs, but her wants – consistently and time after time. A measurable, customer driven, prevention-oriented and an essential requirement of TQM.

Consistent Quality. Right every time, not just the first time.

Consultant. An individual with skills to define and identify group dynamics and ownership for the improvement process, and who can analyse, plan and influence change. He or she provides options on what can be done to move ahead.

Control Chart. Diagramatic representation of the results of an analysis of data obtained in the running of a process. The most common form of control chart is shown below and is the result of statistical analysis of process data represented in a way that shows if the process is under control or not.

194

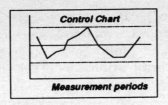

COQ. See Cost of Quality. Also a fried hen. Goes well with au vin.

Corrective Action Team. A group or team formed by management for quality improvement, usually in response to a clearly identified problem which requires correction. See also Project Team.

Cost of Quality. Cost of quality is total labour, materials and overhead costs which are attributed to:

1. Preventing non-conformance of output.
2. Appraising output to ensure conformance to requirements.
3. Correcting or scrapping non-conforming input or output.

Major categories are:

Appraisal. Inspecting output to detect non-conformance and auditing conformance.

Prevention. Actions to ensure that it is done right every time.

Failure. Correcting or scrapping non-conformance both internally and externally.

Required Work. All work not defined as prevention, appraisal or failure. (Any function that, if eliminated, will result in all (100%) of output not conforming to requirements). By definition, required work is not a cost of quality.

Critical Quality Issue. A list of quality improvement opportunities that are developed from analysis of the strategic business plan, customer acceptance reports, cost of quality, or employee perception and attitude data.

Critical Success Factors. A series of past tense, single focus statements that describe **measurable** results characterising the organisation when the vision is being achieved.

CSF. See Critical Success Factors.

Customers (External). The reason your organisation exists. An organisation or person who buys from another. When services are involved, the purchaser is often called a 'client'.

195

Customers (Internal). All the employees of the organisation.

Demonstration Project. A project specifically selected to demonstrate the quality improvement process.

Employee Job Certification. Evidence that shows the employee is capable of performing to specifications and expectations of a specific job function or position. This includes periodic re-certification and training to correct deficiencies. Employee Job Certification is a vital component of total quality in service and product operations and can be applied to all areas of a business.

Error Prevention (Control).

Detection. Inspection by various methods, which generally leads to specification conformance.

Prevention. Identifying expectations and fixing problems that keep people, equipment and systems from performing to expectations; ultimately leads to increased productivity, reduced costs, more profits and management of a process or a target.

Error Sources. Lack of quality is due to errors that are:
1. Management controllable.
2. Operator controllable.

Both types of errors contain error subspecies:
1. Errors which are accidental or careless.
2. Errors due to lack of technique.
3. Wilful errors.

Errors/Mistakes. The presence of error indicates lack of conformance, defects, a deviation from expectations. The presence of variation from the true value can imply carelessness, wilful errors, or management system problems.

Expectations. A combination of written specifications and emotional needs (wants). The customer will consider expectations to be reasonable, due, or necessary.

External Customer Sensitivity. Defining sources of data that can be generated by customer contact, third parties, sales, marketing technical service, competitive analysis, surveys, sales adjustments and complaints. Used to evaluate and measure current levels of customer satisfaction.

FA. See Functional Analysis.

Facilitator Network. A pool of skilled facilitators who foster and boost the disciplines necessary to implement the improvement process.

Fishbone Diagram. See Cause and Effect Diagram.

Flow Chart. A pictorial representation of the steps which constitute a process. Different shapes of box represent different types of activity.

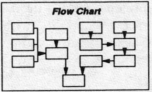

Focused Interviews. A structured, facilitated discussion that serves as a tool for collecting ideas and insights from all levels, and which can reveal the need or opportunity for improvement.

Functional Analysis. A process for identifying quality improvement opportunities within a department, project or operation. Particularly well suited for support and service functions.

Gantt Chart. A diagrammatic representation of actions spread over a time period.

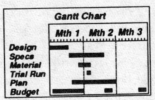

Goal Setting. Short- and long-term goals that provide meaningful, realistic stepping stones to the ultimate objective.

Graph. A tool in the form of a drawing that exhibits a functional relationship between two sets of numbers. Used to organise data into pictorial form, and often shows no relationship. An example is a line diagram:

197

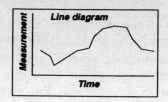

Histogram. A plot of a frequency distribution in the form of rectangles whose bases are equal to the cell interval and whose areas (heights) are proportional to the frequencies. Widely used to compare process capability with tolerance limits. Exhibits measures of central tendency and dispersion.

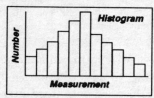

Impact-COQ Improvement. The results of a project that reduces Cost of Quality for an organisation. Real impact will come initially by reducing internal and external failure and appraisal cost.

Impact-Other. The results of a project that will affect suppliers, employees, distributors or customers. This impact should improve the organisation's competitive edge.

Improvement Projects. Smaller projects; department oriented; top down direction.

Ishikawa Diagram. See Cause and Effect Diagram.

Just-in-Time (JIT).

Narrow Sense. A manufacturing process where all activities take place such that only the required material is at a necessary place at the necessary time.

Broad Sense. Just-in-Time refers to all activities of manufacturing which make the Just-In-Time movement of material possible, i.e. no stock production.

Management Acceptance of Error. A major deterrent to satisfying customer's expectations is management acceptance of less than 100% conformance. In technical terms, these are referred to as AQL's, acceptable quality levels, % defective, defects in parts per million and so on. In many cases the actual level of error accepted is delegated to the quality department, effectively shielding management from recognising its true extent.

Management Commitment to Quality. Commitment means to put in charge, trust, to bring about or perform an agreement and a pledge. Effective commitment goes beyond words. There must be a plan to achieve the destination of quality improvement and a method to deploy the plan of action.

Market Niche Quality. The provision to satisfy customer wants over and above customer needs (commodity quality), so that your product or service is differentiated in the market.

Measurement Indices. The numeric measure used to guide the search for better performance. Recognised as a means rather than an end.

Mentor (see Champion). A highly placed person, who can operate behind the scenes, to give support and guidance to visible team leaders of the quality process or to a project team. This person is knowledgeable in the culture of the organisation, is trusted as a counsellor or coach, and is able to open doors and remove barricades to progress.

NGT. See Nominal Group Technique.

Nominal Group Technique. A data collection and consensus-forming methodology involving groups of people selecting ideas, facts or suggestions, grouping them according to type and voting to produce an order of priority.

Objective. What is specifically to be accomplished on a quality improvement project.

Pareto Diagram. Displays the vital few and the important many. The diagram visually shows by cumulative frequency in a histogram, the top few failures that cover most of the cost.

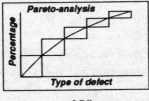

Personal Accountability for Quality. The concept that everyone has a customer and provides a product or service to that customer, and in turn is the customer of another person. The quality of performance by each individual, and the acceptance of responsibility for quality, can then be described as 'quality at the source'.

Positive Action Request (PAR). Employee-originated requests pointing out obstacles that prevent achievement of 100% conformance.

Process. A sequence of functions characterised as having:
1. Measurable input.
2. Value-added tasks.
3. Measurable output.
4. Repeatable steps.

Function. One of a group of related actions resulting in an output.

Output. Things and information that are the end result of a function.

Input. Items and information that are required to perform a function.

Value-added-Function. An action that transforms an input into an output which is more useful to the internal or external customer.

Supplier. A provider of input.

Task. The smallest unit of people's actions or behaviour which is practical or reasonable to study, qualify, or analyse.

Process Capability (Theoretical). The limits within which a tool or process operates based upon minimum variability as governed by prevailing circumstances, such as one operator, one source of raw materials, etc.

Project. A quality improvement project on a specific product, service, or process where the objective is a breakthrough in knowledge to improve from historical levels of performance to a new level considerably better than the existing level. See also Demonstration Project.

Project Team. A team with authority from the Quality Steering Team or management to utilise resources of all kinds to accomplish a specific project. The project team may not be authorised to correct a problem but simply to study the problem and **advise** on the options available for correction. In such cases the word **advise** would appear in the project title. See also Corrective Action Team.

Project Team Leader. A highly skilled and respected person, who is given direct authority from the Quality Steering Team or management to assemble a team and utilise resources of all kinds to accomplish a specific project.

Pull System. The production of items only as demanded for use or to replace those taken for use.

QC. See Quality Circles.

QIP. See Quality Improvement Project.

QIT. See Quality Improvement Team

QST. See Quality Steering Team

Quality Action Team. See also Corrective Action Team

Quality Assurance. All those planned or systematic actions to provide adequate confidence that the product or service will satisfy the customer. The activity of providing all concerned with the evidence needed to establish the confidence that the quality control function is being performed adequately. To ensure quality in a product so that the customer can buy it with confidence and use it for a long period of time with confidence and satisfaction. Quality Assurance is the essence of quality control and strongly directed towards new product development.

Quality at the Source. A quality control method that requires each operator to be trained, provided with tools to achieve self control, and take responsibility for the quality of the product produced. The focus is on defect prevention, not detection.

Quality Awareness. The actions necessary to make sure everyone has a realisation, perception or knowledge of where the organisation stands on quality. The words and deeds that help the new quality attitude.

Quality Characteristics. To the customer, a quality characteristic is the basic building block of quality. It describes a feature or property of the product, material or service, that is

201

needed to achieve functionality and therefore conformance to expectations. To a producer, a quality characteristic is a translation or substitution of the customer's requirements, and appears as a specification which has a target and range.

Quality Circles. Employee involvement groups typically have the same job responsibilities. The participants are taught problem solving and brainstorming skills by facilitators. Quality Circles are generally voluntary. Work centre teams, which use the problem solving techniques, are usually not voluntary.

Quality Control. The operational techniques and the activities which sustain a quality of product or service that will satisfy given needs; also the use of such techniques and activities. The regulatory process through which we measure actual quality performance, compare it with standards and act on the difference. To practise quality control is to develop, design, produce and service a quality product or service which is most economical, most useful, and always satisfactory to the customer. Its characteristics include: organisation wide quality control, education and training, Quality Control Audits, utilisation of statistical methods, and nationwide quality control promotion.

Quality Definition. The consistent conformance to customer's expectations.

Quality Emphasis Survey. The survey evaluates the level of implementation and use of total quality management through-out the organisation.

Quality Encounter (Internal). A meeting where members of two departments that operate in a customer/vendor relation-ship discuss mutual quality concerns to determine expectations and define improvements.

Quality Engineering. That branch of engineering which deals with the principles and practise of product and service quality assurance and control.

Quality Events. Organisation sponsored displays of its com-mitment to quality, such as quality commitment days, quality expos, recognition ceremonies.

Quality Improvement Process Facilitator and Network.
The person who fosters an understanding and prepares the plan of action necessary to adapt quality improvement to the organisation's history, values and culture. The network assures that the consultants necessary to foster the quality process are readily available.

Quality Improvement Project. A project run by a project team with well-defined goals and responsibilities to solve or define a specific set of issues or problems.

Quality Improvement Project. Quality improvement becomes real by picking specific projects for change, assigning personnel to work on the projects and establishing measurement indices to record progress.

Quality Improvement Team. See Corrective Action Team. See Project Team.

Quality Improvement Tools. Largely statistical and problem solving in nature, and must be understood by everyone for successful management of total quality.

Quality Incentive Programme. A programme, usually of short duration, designed to compensate the employee for ideas that lead to cost reduction or quality improvement. The focus is usually on the employee, where typically only 15% of the problems originate.

Quality Measurements. Yardsticks of measuring quality improvements. Typical examples are cost of non-conformance (CONC), unit cost of quality, or measurements that define customer's satisfaction.

Quality Policy. A formal written statement from management that everyone can read and understand defining where the organisation stands on quality, and what it expects of the organisation's quality performance.

Quality Steering Team. A group or work pattern of interfacing human and/or machine activities, directed by information, which operates on and/or directs material, information, energy, and/or humans to achieve a common specific purpose or objective.

Quality Systems Survey. A documented activity performed

to verify, by examination and evaluation of objective evidence, that applicable elements of the quality system are suitable and have been developed, documented, and effectively implemented in accordance with specified requirements.

Recognition. To communicate and acknowledge with appreciation the performance of individuals and teams, through highly visible reinforcement of the fact that management supports quality improvement.

Relative Product Quality Analysis. A quantitative assessment of conformance to required product or service expectations from the customer, and in relationship to major competition.

Resource Required. Resources include time spent by personnel on a project as well as money paid to consultants, other organisations or on capital investment.

Role Playing (Adult Learning Process). An effective teaching concept, where the student is involved in a case study and roles are assumed by the participants, who then observe, evaluate, and play out the role of a character.

Scatter Diagram. A tool for studying the correlation of two variables 1 and 2. each point represents a pair of values.

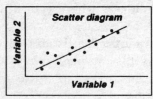

SPC. See Statistical Process Control.

Specifications. A list of essential quality characteristics, with targets and tolerances, usually describing the total allowable variation (tolerance) around a level or state. Can also be defined as the maximum acceptable excursion of a characteristic, as defined by the design engineer's interpretation of the customer's expectations.

Statistical Process Control. A set of statistical techniques, by which actual process fluctuations are compared with historical process data from an in-control situation. The 'amount of control' can be quantified in a so-called 'Process Capability Index' indicating the risk of quality data outside previously defined limits.

Strategic Business Plan. A list of key success factors for a given industry which will, when implemented, allow the organisation to meet corporate performance objectives while competing in that industry's market.

Supplier Qualification (Certification). Certification involves an understanding between the purchaser and supplier regarding product quality and service requirements. Upon a supplier's satisfaction of the purchaser's requirements, the purchaser will suspend testing and inspection and rely on the supplier's quality systems and demonstrated process capability to deliver product meeting all quality and service requirements. Certification is limited to a specific supplier facility, process, service or part as raw material.

Teamwork (Team Building). Work performed by a number of associates, each doing a part to the efficiency of the whole and using a mutually defined method and leading toward a common goal. Also defined as equipping key personnel with the knowledge and skills to build team structures within functions, departments or divisions.

Total Quality Control. An effective system for integrating the quality development, quality maintenance and quality improvement efforts of the various groups in an organisation. Enables production and service at the most economical levels which allows full customer satisfaction. Organisation wide quality control means that everyone in every division in the organisation must study, practise and participate in quality control (See Quality Control definition).

Total Quality Management (The Definition). A management philosophy focusing on customers' expectations, preventing problems, building commitment to quality in the entire work force, and promoting open decision making.

Total Quality Management (The System). The collection of activities in the Total Quality Management process which, taken together as a whole, perform as one vital function.

TQM. See Total Quality Management

Vision Statement. A statement from the organisation on what it wants to be in about 5 years time. It shows direction. It is a tool to position the customers' perception about the organisation and the organisation's image of itself. It is a goal for each part of the organisation to create a quality improvement to achieve.

Workshop. Experience learning processes using adult learning theory and practise. Examples are role playing, observing, presenting, discussing and interactive hands-on situations that best simulate your work and business environment.

Slice 95 Bibliography

1. Right First Time, Frank Price, Wildwood House, 1986.
2. The Quality Gurus, Department of Trade and Industry (UK).
3. Quality through People, John Choppin,
4. Total Quality Management, John Oakland, University of Bradford.
5. Leadership and the One Minute Manager, Blanchard et al, Willow Books.
6. Juran's Quality Control Handbook, Fourth Edition, Joseph Juran, McGraw-Hill,
7. Best Practice Benchmarking, Department of Trade and Industry (UK).
8. The Case for Quality Costing, Department of Trade and Industry (UK).
9. The Industrial Society, North West Quality Club meetings.
10. Quality Without Tears, Philip B Crosby, McGraw-Hill, 1986.
11. Making Things Happen, John Harvey-Jones,
12. Animal Farm, George Orwell,
13. Thriving on Chaos, Tom Peters,
14. In Search of Excellence, Tom Peters,
15. Bywater Technology, Quality Management Services, Chertsey, Surrey.
16. The Gamesman, Michael Macoby,
17. Quality Improvement Barriers, Quality Progress, July 1991.
18. The European Quality Award. European Foundation for Quality Management, Eindhoven, the Netherlands.
19. Delco Electronics booklet on FMEA, Liverpool, UK.
20. Managing Change by Changing Management, British Institute of Management Essay, Richard Varey, Management Today, December 1991, Page 5.

21. Quality Assurance, the route to efficiency and competitiveness, Lionel Stebbing, Ellis Horwood Limited, Chichester, England.

22. Out of the Crisis, W. Edwards Deming, Cambridge University Press, 1982.

23. Managing for the Future, Peter F. Drucker, BCA, Butterworth Heinemann, Oxford, UK, 1992.

24. Power-Creating it, Using it, Helga Drummond, BCA, Kogan Page Limited, London, UK, 1992

25. Zapp, the Lightning of Empowerment, William C. Byham, et al, Random Century, London, 1991.

26. The Seven Habits of Highly Effective People, Stephen R. Covey, Simon and Schuster, New York, USA, 1989.

27. Continuous Quality Improvement Booklet, York MDM, King Street, Leeds, UK.

Index